reflections of a life **up north**

reflections of a life **up north**

by Deborah Wyatt Fellows

foreword by Kurt Luedtke

Prism Publications, Inc.
Traverse City, Michigan

thank you

To my parents, who drove us North and helped me chase a dream.

To the staff and friends who have sustained *Traverse, Northern Michigan's Magazine* since its earliest days, and thus made possible this book.

To the readers of the magazine, who have taught me, sometimes poetically, always passionately, how universal the celebration of Up North really is.

To those who work for the future of Northern Michigan's land and water, without whose efforts the life we all cherish will be lost.

To Ben, Peter, Austin and Olivia, for being such good sports about appearing in some columns and for letting me tag along to see childhood in Northern Michigan all over again.

And to Neal, who weathers the magazine's ups and downs with me, and who's shown me that part of life's ride is joy.

Deb Fellows

contents

about this book

The summers of a childhood can make memories so suffused with light, so saturated by color, that the yearnings they foster reach into a life, get hold of it, give it shape the way a mold forms liquid metal.

This is a book about one woman's sense of where she lives, a portrait made of words and photographs from the magazine she created so as to earn a living in a place she would not leave.

The place that got its hooks into Deb Wyatt is a part of what people in Michigan call Up North, an area carved by the advance of the glaciers and soothed by their retreat.  Bordered and defined by its lakes, it's a region of surpassing beauty and is thus endangered: appetites to preserve or develop the land compete for a future that will be largely decided by the farmers whose willingness and ability to hang on to their ever more valuable fields and orchards are already sorely tested.

It's twenty-five years since Deb came back from Chicago to live again where she had lived in the summers of her youth and where she now accepted a position in magazine management by founding one. Thoughtfully, she named it *Traverse the Magazine,* as if claiming that there was such a thing might make it so.

Unsurprisingly, *Traverse* was an immediate failure: it was not news, to me, anyway, that the northwest Michigan market might not be rich enough to support a magazine of any ambition. Of necessity, the staff had day jobs, as did its founder (Soup with that? Salad?). Money was owed everywhere, tears were shed, pledges and promises made and broken, resignations accepted. I watched from the sidelines, a friend, never an investor, and didn't say told-you-so because I hadn't, and in any case, things were tough enough. *Traverse* failed and failed and failed again. For years.

And then one year it didn't. For one thing, the magazine had learned some things: how to operate on tiny margins, how to deal with the boom and bust cycles of a tourist economy. For another, the book was always getting better; money that might have been taken as profit was instead invested in editorial improvement. But there was something more:

Traverse hoped to survive and one day prosper by celebrating an extraordinary part of the country which in fact might benefit more from anonymity; the argument could be made that *Traverse* might best serve the land it claimed to love by shutting up about it, going out of business, as it were.

Deb is the compass that has allowed the magazine to navigate in these waters. Month by month, issue by issue, *Traverse* has so venerated the region that is its reason for being that cynicism is impossible. The intentions of the magazine are pristine and unmistakable and its soul is comprised of the columns which Deb has written over the years, some of which are at the heart of this book.

(I should acknowledge that some of those columns have been spiffed up for their reappearance here. This has to do with the—how to put this?—velocity with which they were originally written, by which I mean that the columns were sometimes—how to put this?—composed later rather than earlier in the production cycle. Ask not to see the sausage made.)

There have been changes over the years. *Traverse the Magazine* is today *Traverse, Northern Michigan's Magazine,* and, coming up on a quarter-century, is both profitable and esteemed; a few months ago, the City and Regional Magazine Association gave it a gold medal: best in the nation among America's smaller magazines. And Deb Wyatt is now Deb Fellows and the Fellowses appear to be boy-makers, of which there are three.

There is a fourth child, a daughter, and if perchance your day is not going well, I think I can turn that around for you:

Imagine that you are a baby girl, eleven months, bound in swaddling clothes in the Russian manner, staring at the ceiling of the St. Petersburg orphanage where you're in residence. True, you have a roof over your head but your prospects are not bright: you are so tiny that the usual measurements that would assess whether you are damaged or merely unnurtured aren't possible; if somebody's shopping for a certifiably healthy kid, you ain't it.

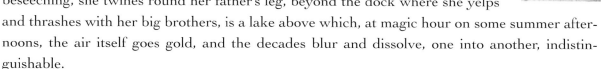

Imagine now that looming over you, tears in their eyes, they are that glad to see you—or sad; how would you know?—are a tall woman and her husband who for reasons of their own propose to take you up, transport you far, far away, tuck you safe into their lives.

Olivia Fellows resides Up North these days, and to say that she is thriving here is to suggest that the surface of the sun may be warm to the touch. Beyond the porch where she curls into her mother's lap, beyond the lawn on which, beseeching, she twines round her father's leg, beyond the dock where she yelps and thrashes with her big brothers, is a lake above which, at magic hour on some summer afternoons, the air itself goes gold, and the decades blur and dissolve, one into another, indistinguishable.

Most Sundays, Livvy goes to see her grandparents, who live in the village near which Deborah Wyatt Fellows spent her summers as a child. The memories that Livvy will make now, as she goes about her days, may be very like the memories her mother made then, memories which are responsible for this book, and any number of other things.

Imagine that.

Kurt Luedtke

the ways of summer

It was always the smell that told me we were there. True, we had gone through the prolonged neighborhood goodbyes, packed our favorite T-shirts and ridden knee-to-knee in the Olds '98 for four and a half hours. But I never really felt we were there until we unlocked the door and all the mustiness of a winter closed to the world spilled out to greet us. It was the smell of bulky chairs that you sank to the springs in, of a nubby, lavender day bed on the porch that swallowed you up when you lay on it, of double beds standing in a row, covered with faded, flowered bedspreads that a dozen hands had mended. All the secrets of summers past were waiting. It was the start of another summer Up North.

Of all the things I knew to be true as I wandered the still-cool rooms, I knew that life for the next few months would be very different from life at home. For one thing, at the cottage we were wholly nonjudgmental; no one rated the décor, the food or our behavior. And there was no television, save the time my dad brought up a small black and white TV so we could watch a fuzzy Neil Armstrong walk on the moon. Instead, there were early morning excursions when I'd glide the boat onto the lake before the mist had lifted. There were late-night bonfires in the Lake Michigan dunes, bundled against the evening cold and shivering to horror stories. And there were challenges: Who could swim the farthest out in the lake and touch the bottom, even if it meant swimming through the "seaweed"? Who could eat three bowls of Cheerios and then hang upside down from a tree for the longest without throwing up? Strains of the Beach Boys and the Beatles carried onto the screen porch, marathon games of Monopoly lay in waiting on the living room table and, at night, shrieks cut through the crickets' chirping as someone got caught with a handful of hearts.

all the
secrets of
summers
past were
waiting

As the youngest, I spent a fair amount of time on my own and I read voraciously. My nights were filled with the fantasy of Rudyard Kipling and the mystery of Victoria Holt. I'd lie down on the porch in the early evening and struggle to pick out the words as dusk set in. Someone would inevitably turn on the porch light, inviting the constant, oddly comforting sound of moths struggling against the screen, questing for the light. When we were Up North, no one told me to go to bed. I could drift off to sleep on the porch, *The Swiss Family Robinson* on my chest.

One summer, I discovered an old book collection that was given to my grandmother as a girl in the 1890s. The main character, a young girl named Elsie Dinsmore, led a horrible life filled with evil cousins, cold grandparents, the Ku Klux Klan, an uninterested father and a loving "Mammy." Night after night I devoured the heartbreaking tales of Elsie's life. Sometimes there was nothing to do but put the book down and sob. It was at those times that my mom would intervene. As we wound through canopied county roads in search of ice cream, I would choke out an explanation of what horrible injustice had been done to Elsie. By the time we reached the small harbor town, all that remained of Elsie's world was a swollen face and tear-stained T-shirt.

Some people might question the trauma wrought by Elsie Dinsmore books as opposed to, say, TV's Brady Bunch, whose most upsetting predicament had to do with too many kids for too few

bathrooms. But, despite the enormous amount of ice cream my mom had to buy that summer, she supported my interest in Elsie and old books in general. On trips to Traverse City, we always included a stop at Arnold's Book Store; even though I was only 10, they treated me as a worthy customer. As gentle as I was with the aged books, their spines still cracked as I opened them to peer at the dates, the etchings and, of course, the inscriptions. To this day, the smell of an old book brings memories of a slightly musty day bed and the rhythmic waltz of moths on the screen.

Just as I was trying to figure out why Elsie would marry her father's best friend, my summertime best buddy informed me that I was probably the only girl in the state who was to start sixth grade not wearing a bra. At the time, I was sitting about 20 feet up in a tree with a couple of scabs on my knee and a Band-Aid on my chin. I was stunned, not so much that this disgrace was about to befall me as that I had been completely oblivious to it. My mother, who stopped just short of agreeing with my brother that my figure resembled a No. 2 pencil, reluctantly agreed to bypass Arnold's and followed my determined lead to Milliken's lingerie department. I emerged duly equipped in a "training bra," and assured my friend that I was certain to be out of training by the time I started sixth grade. I wore it faithfully until she went home, then returned it to its box to await its debut in September. At the cottage, I could pretend that time stands still.

Each Friday, my dad would deposit a gaggle of gangling adolescents at the cottage doorstep, friends from downstate coming north for an adventure. It was always a treat when his cargo included my friend Carol. Stoked with neighborhood gossip, she was a connection to a world that seemed far away—one I was never sure I wanted. One summer she reported on a Campfire Girls slumber party, on soldiers patrolling Detroit during the riots and on a new television show called "The Mod Squad."

Then it was my turn. I had gone in the swampy part of the lake to retrieve the rowboat paddle and emerged with no less than six bloodsuckers on one leg, and my brother had to pour salt on them to get them off. There was the neighborhood barbecue when we put on an aquatics show. Wearing her two-piece suit, my oldest sister skied past on one ski, waving to the crowd with both hands, the tow bar behind her knee. I had been to Cypress Gardens the year before and assured Carol that nothing could compare to this. My brother, not to be outdone, came by having wedged his head through the tow bar, waving both hands with the rope around his neck. My mother's frozen smile as she put down her chicken, walked to the end of the dock and waved my siblings to shore meant there were some lines not crossed, even Up North.

By the end of Carol's stay, we'd forgotten about the Campfire Girls and the riots. That was reality; summertime Up North was pure fantasy, and hard as I tried, I just couldn't hold on to it.

Knowing that cottage life wouldn't survive at home only made the summers more precious. As a family we would say that this year we would play more card games at home, we'd get that Monopoly game off the shelf in the basement. But the knot in my stomach on the day we were to leave, that very real ache in my heart as I stood on the dock for the last time, told me it wouldn't be the same tomorrow.

honeymoon at sea

Some people are blessed with a sense of direction. I'm not one of them. Whatever is in front of me is north; forget east or west. Given how much time I spend in the woods, this is worrisome, but the real problem is, I forget that it's true. I regularly believe that I know where I am going. And that, coupled with my ability to persuade, can cause real problems.

I hadn't known Neal all that long before we married, eight months or so. We'd had a few outings gone awry when, new to my turf, he followed my lead. One bike ride meant to cover about four or five miles ended in the dark after close to 20. It was a caution light about my navigating, I'm sure, but unfortunately, it wasn't flashing red.

Thus we found ourselves in a bit of trouble on the last day of our honeymoon on Drummond Island. The day started with a four-hour rental of a 16-foot aluminum boat, a 15-horsepower engine and a picnic lunch. It ended 10 hours later. We had spent the morning casually cruising among the smaller islands off Drummond when sometime after noon we noticed a thick fogbank moving through a channel between islands. So quickly did it move that it caught us as we raced for land. In an instant we were completely engulfed in a fog the color of eggshells, unable to see an outstretched hand.

A very small curtain lifted, just enough for us to see an island not far away. We pulled the boat onto the rocky shore just as the fog closed in again, and we ate our lunch joking about conserving our food in case we were marooned. There was no sign of civilization in any direction. Again the fog lifted so we decided to keep moving, but no sooner had we started than we were sent scurrying back to shore just in front of more fog. This time there were fewer laughs. And this time, the fog didn't lift.

> the fog
> caught us
> as we raced
> for shore

After a while, Neal decided we could wait no longer to prepare for a night in the wild. Off he went with a Boy Scout's sense of purpose, mixed, I know, with a backpacker's glee. There was shelter to seek, berries to pick. I stayed with the boat. Enough time passed that I was imagining the searchlights that would wake us staring down from the Coast Guard helicopter, when suddenly out of the heavy mist an island appeared just a few miles across the channel. I hastily got out the sketchy, Xeroxed map that came with our boat. Before Neal could return with firewood, I had pieced together all the details of where we'd been, where we were and where we needed to be. He was hesitant when I pointed to the island across from us, assuring him that once around it we would see Drummond. As I've mentioned, I can be very convincing.

We were halfway across the channel before the swells grew taller than our boat and the notorious chop of the Great Lakes took hold. The little motor strained each time it left the water, the swells threw buckets of cold water into the boat. Neal yelled continually for me to "Get down!" and I, with exaggerated calm, continually assured him that all would be fine, a performance he neither believed nor appreciated.

Thankful to reach the opposite shore alive, we now were faced with choices equally bad: wilderness to the left and wilderness to the right. I suggested left, certain that just around the bend we would see a cluster of small islands including Drummond in the distance. Our turn around the bend revealed only another desolate point.

"This is it," Neal said. "We stop here."

"One more point," I urged, turning the map slightly to better suit my reasoning.

"One more," he said, noting that our gas would not allow us to go much further anyway. As we rounded the next point we were at the mouth of a breathtaking bay, at the base of which was a small cluster of buildings. We set off with vigor toward the flag that flew in the small harbor. We traveled several hundred more yards before we could make out which flag it was: Canada's. We had crossed the Lake Huron channel.

Cockburn Island has a year-round population of two, a summer population of approximately 75 and once, at the turn of the century, a population of 1,000. We learned all this from Jack Curtis, a delightful man who offered us beer and regaled us with stories of his years working up in Hudson Bay. We also learned that had we turned right once we'd made it across the channel, we would have traveled until we ran out of gas and never seen another soul.

As we followed in the wake of our lodge's much larger boat back toward Drummond Island, Neal informed me that he would never again listen to my directions. Truth be told, I rather hope that's true.

estelle's hill

I came upon him suddenly as I loped up the two-track in a race with the moon. I traveled a path edged by cedars and blocked in shadow; twilight was nearly upon me. He appeared in the half-light, his broad figure moving forcefully despite his struggle to negotiate the snow-covered path in his galoshes. I'm not sure who was more surprised to come upon whom. I'd climbed this hill a dozen times in the last year and had never seen a soul. I would learn he hadn't set foot here in more than two years.

He wore a tweed hat that shaded his eyes and left his ears exposed; his heavy wool coat suggested a conservative sensibility. I apologized for being on his land; he was merely puzzled about why I was there. When I told him it was to get a look at the rising moon, his face softened perceptibly, and he turned without a word to walk up with me.

I tried to assess the man who owned this wonderful hilltop—a magical place where it was possible to watch the sun set and the moon rise together. I wondered what it was he would build on the hill.

The top layer of the earth was soft under our footsteps and the scent of an impending spring floated from the imprints. His shortened breaths mixed with abbreviated phrases and I learned something of him. He was a retired naval officer and he had traveled from Ohio to put his land up for sale. He didn't call it "my land" however; he called it "Estelle's hill." Estelle, his wife of 47 years, had died two years before, before they could build their dream house, the house she had designed from hundreds of magazine pictures that now lay dormant in a file labeled "Our House on the Hill." We walked the last part of the climb in silence.

> he turned
> without a
> word to
> walk up
> with me

The late winter day had been crystal clear. There was just a whisper of a cold wind that nudged at our necks and made us bob from foot to foot in an awkward harmony. In the west, the sun was going down in a shower of color thrown across the midnight-blue sky. The night would be cold and clear. We turned to the east and saw just the tip of the moon's flawless orange symmetry. I told him we were in for a treat. He smiled, but it was a slow smile. We watched in silence.

I asked about the house. Silhouetted by the now-looming presence of the moon, he told me they had owned the land for nearly 15 years, and Estelle had stood on this spot over and over, plotting their future. She could see the house, he said, but he never really could. She would have him pace off the rooms, then stand sturdy as a roof beam as she described room upon room. He smiled recalling how she'd say he could pace off the Great Wall of China to the inch. They had always planned to build in the spring as soon as the ground thawed, he continued. But whenever spring came, Estelle would decide they should wait a bit, until the season's new life had been given a chance to get on its feet. And then he said with a smile, it was always too peaceful or too beautiful to disrupt.

The moon was a perfect white sphere and the ground had turned hard when he said he'd decided to hang onto the land for a while. I felt myself relax. I looked out at the landscape, nestled like a child under its thin and fraying blanket of snow. "You're safe," I whispered with the hope and helplessness of a parent.

As we said goodbye, his decision seemed to sit well with him, and I suspect he knew it would have felt right to Estelle as well. She seemed like someone who would have liked it that people climbed her hill to get closer to the moon.

a christening

I overslept this morning. Usually I am well into my day by the time first light creeps over the hill behind the house. Dawn always seems to happen while I'm in the shower. But this morning I opened my eyes as the barren trees began to glisten on their eastern sides, black bark wet with a night's rain. I watched the browned meadow grass begin to glow, lit by a shaft of morning sun breaking through clouds the color of gunmetal. In the heart of it all, 25 yards from my window, four deer picked their way gracefully across the slope. I had seen five just a few evenings before and was reminded: It's bow-hunting season.

Neal was out of town. I thought about waking my son, Ben, to show him the deer, but he is oblivious to anything outside the smiling faces he now knows, his Johnny Jump Up and, of course, his food source. He slept peacefully next to me as the deer froze, staring intently through our bedroom window as if they'd heard the dog heaving a sigh on her side of the bed. Ben stirred slightly as the deer, satisfied there was no danger, sauntered into the woods.

I lay thinking about the pledge I had made with a small group of family and friends the night before. We'd gathered at the tiny Omena Presbyterian Church to agree to nurture Ben's spirit. It was a blustery, rainy night, already dark at 5:30. As we rounded the curve, the church glowed warm, greeting us in much the same way it has greeted others for generations. Built in 1858, the one-room church has been preserved in its original state through painstaking effort. Betty Armstrong, the Clerk of Session and a member of the congregation since her childhood, had graciously agreed to re-open the church for us; it normally closes each year just after Labor Day. Summer parishioners return to their churches at home and local residents move to pews at other churches around the county. The church was cold inside when we arrived—there is an old heater but it takes an entire day to heat the building, and the heaters Betty brought were not the right voltage. Undeterred, she'd lit candles and prepared for the service.

> we were
> there to
> celebrate the
> concept
> of spirit

As I looked at the faces of our small group, all people I love, bundled in sweaters and jackets and smiling in the light thrown from old chandeliers, I thought how fitting it was that we were in such a lovely, simple building with such history and few conveniences. We were there to celebrate the concept of spirit and, in its purest form, the spirit of Northern Michigan has little to do with conveniences. It has to do with simplicity, natural beauty, community, time with the people we love, respect for the land and water. It has to do with the peace that comes with the dawn.

As a trusting, smiling Ben was handed to my sister and brother-in-law and water was sprinkled on his head, I cast about for how I would define for him—had he been old enough to understand—where I've found a sense of spirit in life. I remembered a morning last spring, about a month before he was born. I topped a hill a mile or so from my house and came upon three horses, one white, two dark, that had gotten out of a neighbor's pasture. I had passed these horses for years as they grazed within the fence. I never pictured them free.

Yet there they were, liberated, racing with the cool wind. They ran through the fields almost as one with such fierceness that for a moment I worried for their safety; they might stumble and all come down at once. I needn't have worried. They dodged and veered with an instinct I could only envy.

Those horses embodied in a moment the life I find here. It is as real as the wind in their manes, in the deer outside my window, in the people I love gathered in a tiny, simple church. It's a quality that I find hard to express in conversations about change and growth in this region. When it comes to things spiritual, people find what they need in the way that is right for them. And it is hard to convince some people that once we have completely blanketed this region in buildings and pavement, the spirit that so many of us find in this place will be gone. Sadly, the fields in which those horses ran free are slated to house a gas station and convenience store, unless my township's residents vote against the rezoning in a special election. If others had seen those horses run free, they could never cover that land with asphalt.

My spiritual life has become inextricably linked to the life that I have known here. Last night, I wished the same for Ben.

fate at the 45th parallel

I have a favorite island story. I've forgotten who told it to me; he's lost in hundreds of late-night tavern conversations. He told me of his great-grandfather, a fruit farmer in Germany, who left his homeland as a young man and traveled by boat to New York. Once there, he asked among the ship captains heading west if anyone could get him near the 45th Parallel. Born on the 45th in Germany, he knew that if he settled in America on that same line, he could grow fruit.

One captain, setting off through the St. Lawrence, bound for Lake Michigan and beyond, told the young man he could get him close. After a lengthy journey the ship docked at South Manitou Island. As the inhabitants of the island hustled to restock the ship's food supplies and load wood for refueling, the captain called to the young man that this was about as close as he would get to the 45th. Hastily, the man gathered his belongings and jumped from the ship.

Unbeknownst to the young immigrant, a woman nearly his age traveling with her parents had had her eye on him. Seeing him leaving, she pulled together her few belongings and jumped off after him. The two were married by another ship captain sometime later and went on to build a life as fruit farmers, first on South Manitou and then in Leelanau County, where their descendants live today.

Sometimes in late fall, when I look out over the expanse of water between the islands and the mainland, I imagine Indians in birch bark canoes crossing to their winter camps. I think about the sudden swirl of activity and the buzz of excitement the island settlers must have felt as a ship approached on the horizon. But mostly I picture a young couple, practically strangers to each other, standing on the shores of South Manitou, watching their ship pull away, leaving them to their fate and future.

bridges crossed

My bedtime reading last night was from a battered, nine-by-six Mead notebook. Written in black magic marker on the cover are the words "Guest Book of Seven Bridges Beginning July, 1987."

The notes, written mostly in pencil by people from across the country, reflect a love affair with a breathtaking piece of property, a magical jumble of rushing rivers and handmade bridges.

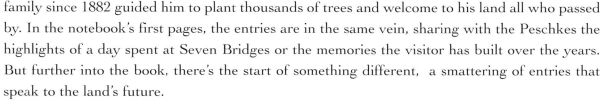

"My young son caught six trout today. He'll remember this spot for as long as he lives. Thanks for letting us borrow it for the morning! All trout were returned in good shape for someone else to enjoy."

"When I'm alone on a stream in the woods, it's the only time I can find serenity without loneliness. This, I would say, is the most beautiful place on Earth … And I've seen more than a few. Thank you."

Who are they thanking? Gordon Peschke, a tool-shop supervisor from Detroit, whose selfless passion for a piece of property that had been in his family since 1882 guided him to plant thousands of trees and welcome to his land all who passed by. In the notebook's first pages, the entries are in the same vein, sharing with the Peschkes the highlights of a day spent at Seven Bridges or the memories the visitor has built over the years. But further into the book, there's the start of something different, a smattering of entries that speak to the land's future.

"More than 20 years since we first came to Seven Bridges, we had a family picture taken here in August of '86. One of our favorite spots. This place is good for the soul. I hope the new owners treasure it."

"I have been coming to the Seven Bridges often for 13 years. And every trip here is always a new experience for me … The solitude and beauty have helped me find many answers to my questions of life. I will come here forever if possible. But now I see it's up for sale. Please—if possible—do not let this place be closed off to the public. There are people such as myself who would lose more than a safe hideaway. We would lose a chance to find the peace in our souls that this place brings to us."

> family
> pressure
> had put
> Seven
> Bridges on
> the market

Family pressure had caused Gordon, then in his late 70s, to put Seven Bridges on the market. The property sold, and a large development was planned. The deal, his wife Cece recalls, broke Gordon's heart. "At that point he couldn't do anything about it. We still came up every summer [from Detroit] to see friends and we would drive by. But I couldn't get him out of the car. He'd just look straight ahead with a big lump in his throat. I'd tell him, 'Look, honey, your work is here. You're leaving a good thing behind. You'll go on living here forever in the 3,000 trees that have sprung from your hands.'" But her words were in vain. Gordon never walked the bridges again.

It was the small pink flags slicing the 291 acres into 10-acre lots, each with river frontage, that ultimately led to the saving of Seven Bridges. Lou Ann Taylor had visited the property for the first time just a few weeks before she brought her friends to Seven Bridges for a long hike and picnic lunch by the river's edge. The significance of the pink flags and stakes was not lost on these women: Virginia Sorenson was chairwoman of the Grand Traverse Regional Land Conservancy, Taylor was a trustee and Helen Milliken, wife of former Governor Bill Milliken, had long been involved in environmental causes. By the end of the picnic, the three had vowed to do all they could to save Seven Bridges from development.

One obstacle after another was thrown in the path of these determined women and the staff of the Grand Traverse Regional Land Conservancy. But one night, in a last-ditch effort, as a blizzard gathered force in Lansing, a handful of people, including Sorenson, made an impassioned plea to the Natural Resources Trust Fund Board. "We were all captivated," said board member Wendy Potts. "I had just finished reading *The Bridges of Madison County* and was really taken with the photographs of how beautiful this place was." The board voted unanimously to grant the funds to purchase Seven Bridges from the developers. Gordon died the following summer, knowing that Seven Bridges would be saved.

They say an act of kindness often inspires another. I have no doubt that will be one of the legacies of Seven Bridges. In fact, an Englishwoman wrote in Gordon's book, "Thanks for sharing this spot with me. Some people would not be so generous. I owe someone a similar good turn."

When I closed the notebook last night, I lay imagining what sort of entry I would have written in the "Seven Bridges Guestbook." It might have gone like this: "It's Mother's Day 1997, and one of the nicest gifts I got today was the joyful faces and laughter of my family and friends as we explored Seven Bridges. What an adventure it was for our little boys. But it was even something more for my husband. He came of age on the Chesapeake Bay and sometimes he still misses not only the ocean but the rushing rivers of West Virginia, where he passed many a day in his kayak. Today, he found a piece of home. Thank you."

a date with aurora

One evening last November, I was seated by the woodstove, surrounded by the rubble of plastic baby toys I had said we would never own. I had a burp cloth on my shoulder, some sort of half-eaten dinner in front of me and the TV on — a new habit we'd picked up with the baby. As we stared blankly at the screen, a message scrolled across the bottom — the Northern Lights were just beginning.

Neal jumped to his feet with an energy I'd not seen in months. "Let's head to the beach!" he exclaimed.

I looked down at Ben. All I could picture was the snowsuit, the hat, the scarf, the car seat, the potential that his sleep could be even more disrupted, if that were possible.

"Oh, you go ahead," I sighed. "I've seen them before. You haven't."

Neal was dressed for the weather in a flash and out the door, headed to the Lake Michigan beach a mile away. But just as quickly, he was back to get me to my feet and show me the streak of orange light just edging over the hill behind the house, looking for all the world like a winter sunrise. The surreal quality of that light where none should be was a shot of adrenalin, strong enough for me to get the baby ready and into the car, along with Sara, our dog.

As is so often the case in Northern Michigan, we had the entire beach to ourselves. The sky was strewn with wispy streaks of light so bright we could see Sara wandering in the dune grass a hundred yards away. That light alone was breathtaking, and similar to the aurora borealis I'd seen before. But then, quite suddenly the show began: the most stunning, awe-inspiring display, natural or manmade, I've ever seen.

The red horizon we'd seen behind the house was recreated on the opposite horizon across the big lake and what followed was a continuous meeting of the two as they turned into extraordinary lavender, red and blue streaks directly over our heads. After several minutes of the dance between the two horizons, there was a moment's pause, and then it was as if the sky exploded from that apex, as if we were looking into the center of an atomic blast, or maybe the center of the universe itself. Waves of color erupted again and again, toppling over one another in a race from the center, a center which now appeared as a brilliant, eerie white spotlight. Things in nature almost never frighten me, and I'm not a person who ever thinks about the possibility of aliens. But the only thought

Sara crept under the car. I crept closer to Neal.

I had scared me: "It's as if a spaceship is going to emerge from that hole and suck us all up." Sara had crept under the car. I had crept closer to Neal. Even Ben was wide-eyed in his car seat.

Before that night, I thought I had a pretty good idea of just how glorious nature can be. But I didn't. I found out on a Friday night, a burp cloth still on my shoulder under my coat. In the blur of being a new parent I'd almost forgotten what lay just beyond our threshold. I'm so grateful it was still there, waiting for me.

a fondness for gravel

It's April and my husband and I are confronted once again with a longstanding dilemma: To pave or not to pave. Granted, our quandary falls short of the struggle for world peace, but it carries its own moral underpinnings. We didn't move to the country just to cover it with pavement. A dirt-and-gravel driveway looks right, sounds right, even smells right when it's in the country. But it has taken all those combined to keep us from paving our little slice of private access—especially in the spring.

Certainly each season comes with its ups and downs for gravel-driveway owners. Summer with a dirt-and-gravel drive and a one-year-old boy means doggedly trying to convert his red-and-yellow plastic "Cozy Coupe" car into a four-wheel-drive vehicle. And there's the constant anxiety over whether there were just 380 throat-closing stones within his reach a minute ago, or 381. We've seen guests fondly watch little Ben swing his toy golf club only to find themselves moments later picking gravel out of their kneecaps. But few would not sigh at the sense of peace felt when passing under the single arch of hemlocks on a summer evening and heading up the dirt drive framed by the garden, the outbuilding and the back hill covered in wildflowers. There is a symbiotic relationship between all these elements in the warm months that means we could never pave in summer.

Fall is heaven for dirt driveway owners. The drive grows hard and cold and is, for all intents and purposes, paved. Only better. Dirt roads are often at their most beautiful when meandering through fall colors, and our drive is no different. We could never pave in the fall.

Our driveway, a gentle slope in warmer months, becomes the face of Eiger in the winter. Many a visitor has careened down its seemingly innocent face, plunging toward the road, helpless, resigned to his fate. Usually at the last moment, one tire grabs onto a small patch of exposed gravel and the car is brought to an abrupt, sideways halt. Having watched from the porch in frozen horror, we run to offer moral support and chauffeur service to the road.

I have absolutely no science to back this up, but I believe dirt driveways are slicker than paved ones in winter. My theory is, you really can't clean the snow off dirt as effectively as off pavement. Not that our snowplow man doesn't try. He comes from the "pedal to the metal" school of snow plowing. Fully three inches of the surface of our drive-

water-filled ruts could swallow a family of four

way ends up in an enormous snowbank somewhere near the middle of our backyard. We were stunned the first time we came home and surveyed this pile of gravel, snow, forgotten sprinklers, bits of plastic toys, abandoned mittens and anything else that happened to be in the path of his plow. When asked why he felt the need to push this frozen concoction some 25 yards out onto the lawn, he answered that he didn't want to run out of space for the snow as the season wore

on. I thought to myself that all the snows of Kilimanjaro would have to fall on our drive to fill the space he'd allotted. But we don't argue. Anyone who is willing to get up and plow in the pitch black of a winter morning can dream all he wants. And besides, that pile made the perfect sledding hill for our toddler all winter long. The truth is, all winter long our driveway is a picturesque, snowy two-track, a visual postcard of winter in the country, and life slows down a bit every time we come upon it. We've agreed we could never really pave in winter, even if it could be done.

But then we get to April, when water-filled ruts in the drive are deep enough to easily swallow a family of four. Small animals are not safe crossing the driveway. Shoes, even laced, have been sucked right off the wearer's foot. I've considered tethering our son to the house with a long line when he goes out to play making it easier to retrieve him if he falls and his stocky little legs begin to sink. Making it up the drive in the spring is something like being the lead driver on some cable TV show called Men, Trucks and Mud. I gun the engine and work the steering wheel as the truck is flung from side to side, tires whining and screeching, mud flying across the windshield. Ben has taken to squealing gleefully in his car seat and flinging his hands up in the air when we make it to the top. This worries me.

From the top, looking back, I see no sign of gravel. We had an entire truckload dumped on the drive last fall, but the mud has just swallowed it whole. Somewhere, two feet down where all that gravel has undoubtedly settled, there is one heck of a driveway. Summer had better get here soon or we may just start digging—or something worse.

summer's strings

Summer Up North. Even as we are living it, the images seem larger than life. The days stretch into impossibly long twilights, bold spinnakers fly, caught by warm winds that become the stuff of legend, beaches reach untouched for miles, freshwater seas lie forever before us. On hot summer days we plunge below a lake's surface, leaving the world behind. Worries and concerns simply melt away in an aquamarine world grown weightless and silent. Water pure enough to breathe streams through our hair, soaking our scalps until they quiver. Footprints in the sand appear to lead nowhere, but for us, toward the only things that seem to matter. We finish each other's sentences when sharing details of summer Up North: a bonfire at the beach, sweet watermelon eaten on the dock, drifting off under the stars. Our days are filled with a gaiety and a peace we know nowhere else, and we find no contradiction in those two emotions existing side by side.

When catching someone's eye in the height of summer, we so often see our own joy looking back. And yet, as shared as we know those experiences and emotions to be, somehow we each feel we are living in our own slice of paradise.

threads that bind

I lie with my head barely propped on the trunk of a fallen tree. The Platte River steams just slightly and sings a frolicsome song as it edges its way through banks covered in frosted gold. The sky is a canvas of gray, branches of young trees etched upon it like torn black lace.

I am alone in this spot. I bowed out when my husband suggested we hike down a steep hill to take a closer look at the river as I am recovering from a minor back injury. Instead, I watched our son Ben's little red hat bobbing above the backpack as he and Neal disappeared beyond a small knoll. The dog, torn between her sense of adventure and her loyalty to me, gave me one last pleading look, trying to change my mind. I waved her on. I crossed my arms on my chest and drew a deep, cold breath. Slowly, I came to remember what I used to know every day: the peace that comes with being alone in the woods.

It wasn't until I let the sound of the wind nudge my imagination that I realized how much I had come to let the practical world dominate my thoughts. Just a few steps earlier on the trail, we had passed a cedar swamp full of jagged tree trunks rising ominously out of a smoky earth. Neal imagined what it would be like to bring Ben and his friends here some Halloween seven or eight years down the road. He began envisioning small lanterns swinging in the night and grown-ups hiding to jump out and scare the kids. I, on the other hand, saw children stumbling into things, skinned knees, maybe some stitches. By the time we passed through the stumps, I had plans for the long rope I would have the children all hold onto so that we wouldn't lose one of them in the night.

we returned unharmed to our little cabin

But now I remember another cedar swamp, equally ominous, that Neal and I hiked through in the Porcupine Mountains in late autumn, shortly after we were married. We were nearing the end of an 18-mile trek. Hungry and giddy, we followed a spongy path into a field of craggy, threatening dead trees. I had fallen well behind and as I tried to catch up, I watched my feet to be sure I didn't stray into the marsh that surrounded me. My mind ran wild with all manner of things that might play themselves out in a swamp like that.

We returned unharmed to our little cabin in the middle of the mountains, heated by wood and lit only by candles. I awoke in the middle of that night to the sound of Sara wearing a nervous path between the door and me, her patient indicator that she needed to go out. The cabin was so hot that there had been no need for clothes in our down bags. I pulled on my boots and stepped outside in the light of a full harvest moon. It was just fifteen yards to the edge of the river that rushed silver. Steam began rising slowly from my body as my skin's warmth met the

frigid air. My body was as much a part of nature as the river and the rock that gave me a place to sit watching. For a few minutes, I had this powerful, familiar feeling that I was alone in the middle of the world. Just as the cold began to truly get hold of me, I climbed down from the rock and headed back to the cabin. Sara and I entered through the heavy wood door, and Neal stirred at the sound of its creak. The distance from my perch on that rock to the warm cabin marked my first true realization that I was married, that I'd never be really alone in the same way again. I was happy to come in.

From my place along the banks above the Platte, I see a tiny red hat, peeking in and out through the tangled trees in the distance. I hear Sara, still some distance away, breaking through the crisp brush as she hurries toward me.

May you always know the peace of your own company in the woods. And may you always be found again by those you love.

lingering light

I have always been a sunset person. I have dipped my toe in many a sunrise and admit to a hazy pleasure when mixing a strong cup of coffee with the particularly lucid colors of first light. But my heart lies with the evening shades of sunsets Up North.

My first memory of a Lake Michigan sunset begins with a favorite T-shirt, a hand-me-down from my brother, apricot in color with navy stripes and worn so soft the threads were bare in places. I was 10 years old and I wore that shirt to almost all the weekly potlucks in the town hall near our cottage. The tables in the hall were always brimming with family recipes, including peculiar salads I sometimes tried and baked goods I never missed. After everyone was suitably sated, the tables and chairs were pushed back and we roller-skated on the wooden floor. Around and around we'd go until our legs turned to jelly and the people lining the walls, chatting and knitting, blurred into a colorful mosaic. It was after one of those wonderful nights that I was swept up in a throng of older kids making their way to the Big Lake. I was rarely in on such excursions, and I shivered with anticipation and a slight chill off the lake that met us as we walked onto the broad beach. It took no time for a fire to be built, and its dull orange glow grew rich and deep as the sun set at what seemed an arm's length away. Strange hues melded with fire smoke, scary stories and laughter. I dozed eventually, snuggled against my sister, the colors of the sunset playing on my drooping eyelids. It was mystical and magical, and I was completely in awe.

Throughout my 20s, I always walked the sunsets of Northern Michigan with my dog, Sara. Every evening found us walking Lake Michigan beaches, hiking a favorite two-track or just putting our shoulders to a sub-zero wind in a battle of wills. When I bought a farmhouse in the countryside, our walk to Lake Michigan was a one-mile trek down a country road to a dirt road and ultimately to a stunning bay that framed the islands. On the way, Sara would romp and play, hiding in the woods ahead and jumping out when I reached her in an earnest but futile effort to startle me. I always rewarded her with due exclamation.

the world felt wild and mysterious

Unless ice floes barred her from the water, Sara would walk knee deep into the lake and always swim after a casually tossed stick. Invariably, we stayed too late during those many months of fall, winter and spring, when we had miles of beach all to ourselves. The sun would set in a fiery glow and with it would go the last illusion of warmth. Night always caught me off guard. We would start the trek home in purple twilight. For many years, in the "off-season," we could walk right back up the middle of the road, away from the trees, open to the stars as they dove out of an indigo sky rapidly going black. When I reached the house I would turn to the west to see the very last remnants of the sunset lingering in the slow smoke from my chimney. Standing in that extraordinary partial light, the world felt wild and mysterious and absolutely free.

Last night I watched the sun set from a small bench we've placed on the dock at our new house for just that purpose. Neal and I came to the bench after bath time and bedtime rituals for our young sons, Ben and Peter. We were exhausted and came seeking peace, and quiet, and some sort of absolution. The lake was as placid as newly blown glass and seemingly as delicate. A massive, forested slope in the west began to go black as the sun set behind it. I glanced up at the birch trees, still golden in the light, and then up at the house where two little boys lay snuggled under quilts of rabbits and clouds. In that soft light, the world seemed safe and at peace.

Ben went to sleep last night in his favorite Grand Canyon train T-shirt, worn soft as silk, threadbare in places. Thirteen-year-old Sara lay buried a month before under the soft blanket of cedar needles in the grove behind our house. And there was the sun on its timeless trek, still finding its way to Lake Michigan's horizon in a spectacular blaze of color.

zone 5

I had known my husband-to-be only about six months when he told me he wanted to rent a Rototiller. Uh-oh.

Understand that I was about to marry a man who in our brief courtship had already plied me with drawings for a water-borne generator (powered by methane emitted by an underwater composter), a solar-powered kayak and, most recently, a one-man submarine designed to skim the murky bottom of inland lakes. Nor has the memory faded of the evening I came home to find the yard covered in small pieces of newspaper, this the result of his effort to make mulch by pulverizing newspaper in a garbage can with a weed-wacker. A Rototiller in this man's hands was not to be casually embraced. Still, he promised to till nothing larger than something maybe six by twelve. What could go too wrong?

As it turned out, nothing. That little garden plot, which he expanded over the next four years, but only slightly, gave him hours of solitary enjoyment, and provided us with beautiful, evolving swatches of color in the backyard, flowers for the house, food for our table. Never one to rest on his laurels, Neal pored over gardening catalogs each year to reinvent his little plot. At first he was stricken to learn he'd left home in Washington, D.C.—Zone 7 on the growing maps—for Northern Michigan's Zone 5, one which gardeners refer to as "hardy." But he quickly learned that our climate is superb for a perennial garden. The cold winters give bulbs and perennials the dormancy they need to dazzle us each spring and summer. Plants like tulips and daffodils thrive here, though they're almost impossible to grow in more tropical climates.

> we left that farmhouse and its cherished garden

Last fall we left that farmhouse and its cherished garden and moved to a cottage that had been owned by a family from Detroit for 17 years. It was obvious on our first visit to the house that someone in the family was a gardener. A kidney-shaped plot surrounding a weathered wooden flagpole had clearly once been a showcase, though it was now overgrown with waist-high grasses and weeds. Carefully selected plantings bordered the deck and unruly rosebushes climbed the back of the cottage, still brandishing huge, gorgeous blossoms even in mid-October. A nicely tended vegetable garden was tucked behind the garage.

The couple who had spent so many wonderful summers in this spot were brokenhearted to part with their small haven, but their children were grown and scattered, and the wife—a woman as gracious and lovely as the roses she'd tended—had grown ill. With great care, she and her husband tried to tell Neal what they could about the plantings they had nurtured through the years. And while it was a painful parting for them, they seemed to find some peace in the image of more little children running the edges of the garden into which Neal would breathe new life.

As I write, those gardens are nestled under a blanket of snow. But the air is warm and thick, and spring is decidedly on its way. It won't be long until the first crocuses pop and the earth gets warm enough to sink your hands into. And just as Neal and I will pause to remember our small garden plot, certain to be expanded and made their own by the avid gardeners who bought our farmhouse, so I'm sure will the couple whose cottage we've bought picture their gardens springing to life. For all of us—whether in our mind's eye or just outside the window—color and light, laughter and possibility are just around the corner.

shooting the tube

To portage or not to portage, that was the question posed to the occupants of three canoes, all of which had converged at one spot on the Crystal River. Neal, our ever-earnest seven-year-old son, Ben, and two of his friends were in one of the canoes. I paddled with my sister Wendy and my two-year-old, Austin, who had spent the trip thus far perched in the center like a king on the Nile, raining nonstop oratory upon us, including, but not limited to, some very stern commands. He clutched in his chubby little hands an entire bag of corn chips I had given him in an attempt to keep his hands in the boat. Now, at the portage, still stunned by his good fortune, he was concerned only that he not be asked to relinquish his chips. We knew our four-year-old was already through the portage, as along the way we had heard him and his best buddy, Frankie, in a canoe up ahead, singing endless renditions of "Dip, Dip and Swing" with Frankie's parents.

Two young girls just into adolescence piloted the third canoe at the portage, their parents following in canoes with younger children. Multicolored braces gleamed behind nervous smiles as we all discussed the alternative to the portage—shooting our canoes through a culvert. It was an easy choice for Neal. After seeing his charges safely overland, he returned to his canoe, got on his knees in the center and effortlessly shot through the tube. It was a tepid nod to his 20s, a time he spent searching for Class IV whitewater to kayak. He made it look awfully easy, emboldening those of us still on the other side.

By the time Neal returned to retrieve Austin and the corn chips, it was decided: We would all go through the culvert. Turn hard to the left when you come out, Neal instructed, or you'll crash hard into the opposite bank. We didn't really need to hear that.

As Wendy and I held onto a low-hanging branch and the girls held onto our canoe, we discussed who should go first. For reasons I can't remember but hope had not to do with my own cowardice, it was decided the girls would go first. They pushed off, paddled upstream a bit, then turned the canoe and worked hard to get the best straight-on shot they could. Their faces were pictures of determination sprinkled with a healthy dose of fear. They maneuvered the canoe perfectly on the first try (it took us three), pulled their paddles into the canoe at the critical moment and ducked down. They were screaming the moment they entered the tube and

they were screaming the moment they entered

didn't stop till they came out the other side. When my sister and I blasted through, the faces of those two girls on the other side were still flushed with victory. Going through that pipe on their own took courage, confidence and a sense of adventure, and they felt it.

We all gathered on a sandy point to eat picnic lunches in a light mist. The boys took turns sliding through the smooth mud of the river's edge, emboldened by the sight of their bodies painted black like participants in some tribal ritual. The youngest of us sat on worn river rocks and giggled as the gentle flow of water tickled their toes.

We ended the outing in a pouring spring rain that had a chill to it, and surprisingly, there wasn't a complaint in the crowd. Parents began packing up waterlogged belongings and kids. We hadn't had to sign our children up to play that day. We hadn't had to be accepted. It wasn't a competition. The river, like this region's beaches and trails, is virtually free, spectacularly beautiful and always available. And sometimes what's found, I thought as my eye landed on those two girls from the culvert, is a bit of self-esteem to tuck away. And that could make all the difference.

seeing clearly

For a spell last winter, clear skies filled our days with air so cold that the only way to enjoy time outside was to keep moving—fast. The cold brought a bit of snow that was lighter than air, billowing up in intoxicating clouds when you kicked it with a boot. Tree trunks and limbs spent whole weeks encased in ice, shimmering black like Asian pottery.

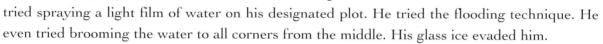

Into this world, Neal provided the perfect complement—an ice rink on the lake. What started as a muse one cold afternoon very quickly became a pursuit, a small quest for the grail. Creating glass ice became his passion. Every night for a week brought a new drawing, a new way to push and pull physics to work in his favor. Then, after the kids went to bed, he began trooping down to the lake in the dark, dragging hoses, brooms, shovels and a light. In sub-zero weather he tried spraying a light film of water on his designated plot. He tried the flooding technique. He even tried brooming the water to all corners from the middle. His glass ice evaded him.

I arrived home from work one night, tired and cringing in the cold as I hurried toward the house. The children were at a friend's house and wouldn't be home for a half hour. I was picturing something, anything, warm and quiet. Neal intercepted me between the car and the house. He was elated. He had ice. Real ice. With a heavy sigh that he appeared to take no notice of, I followed him through the web of paths the kids had carved in the snow. We picked our way down the bank to the lake. A small outdoor floodlight lit a corner of the rink as I stepped onto the small oasis in the ghostly tundra of the lake. I was instantly taken with how beautiful it all was. We slipped and slid in that frosty night air, looking out at the vast night sky over the lake and just the beginnings of stars.

creating glass ice became his passion

Our boys didn't know how to skate, and we'd all but forgotten. I was muttering things less than joyful that first weekend as I laced inflexible hockey skates with fingers frozen from the effort of just getting a small foot into the skate. There was a lot of falling that first day and some of the tears that accompany expectations of finesse. But little by little they moved from tentative steps to hurtling headlong to actually skating. We had all manner of skating days, some in sweaters under a warm sun, some bundled against a north wind that came in a fury from across the lake. There were bonfires, hot dogs, cocoa and one trip to the E.R. for 12 stitches in Peter's chin.

One evening the boys and some friends skated until it was getting too dark to see safely. I was just starting to round them up and move them toward the house when Neal arrived home, two big floodlights in tow. He set them up, flipped them on and the boys, frozen in the sudden glare  for a moment, began leaping about the ice like Stanley Cup victors. Noses running, cheeks flaming, gloves frozen solid, they begged us to let them stay out. As I turned and looked up at the house, I remembered so clearly that sensation of just not being ready to go in on a cold winter night, but liking the knowledge that the warm house would be there when I was.

As February waned and we got a few back-to-back thaws, the re-frozen slush on the rink made it difficult to keep the rink's ice smooth. It looked as if the skating season was coming to an end. Then one sunny Saturday, noticing the blue sheen of smooth ice on the lake itself, we decided to lace up the skates and try our luck on ice beyond the confines of the rink.

We stepped over the mounds of snow that rimmed the rink to reach the open ice. It was very eerie. We huddled together a bit, gawking through 22 inches of ice so clear we could see the depths of the lake below. We crept over the not-very-reassuring cracks in the surface of the ice that ran as far as the eye could see. And then, slowly, we began to skate. And skate we did. Anywhere we wanted to go for as far as we wanted to go. The kids began to howl, skate backwards and attempt sweeping figure-eights never tried within the confines of our small rink. I felt every bit as graceful as Dorothy Hamill set free on a rink the size of which even she would envy. We skated for hours with hats stuffed in pockets and jackets flung open.

As parents we spend a lot of time setting limits for our kids, reining them in, defining their boundaries. That day, as I watched their smiles, their bravery, their hearts bursting with the freedom and magnitude of it all, I realized part of the thrill for me was just letting them go.

spring unshuttered

From a vantage point high above the cottage, Northern Michigan lay before us, drenched in the subdued hues of an Andrew Wyeth painting. It was early April, and the deep green of the cedars and a slight hint of blue to the lake were the only colors to interrupt the ghostly stands of barren birch and poplar.

Dawn was breaking somewhere behind us, so powerfully it was casting soft lavender and orange all the way to the western sky. Fog rose on the lake, making the islands nothing more than faint, gray specters across the eerily calm water. The air was heavy and damp and redolent of the soil. It seeped into our sinuses and settled in our lungs. It smelled of mud and mosses and a natural world straining to emerge.

We looked down at the large white cottage, shuttered tightly against the assaults of winter. It was the cottage my good friend's grandfather had built more than 50 years ago, and she had never seen it in early spring. The family never opened it until late in May. We had arrived an hour before but not gone inside, choosing instead to climb the hill and wait for dawn.

The world seemed wholly at peace. A deceptively warm breeze touched our hair and knelt on the fields, whispering seductively to the earth, trying to tease loose the

mysteries of spring. I could feel the earth, tempted, beginning to soften its winter shell. At midday the ground would be spongy but by evening the surface would harden to steel; the earth knew not to trust the fickle song of the wind. "Soon," the earth seemed to sigh beneath us, soon the winds could be trusted. I longed for such patience.

Dawn's colors had reached the roof of the cottage as we turned the small wooden knobs upright and pulled open heavy, wooden window shutters, painted green. The house groaned and grumbled, crotchety, awakened prematurely from sleep. The rooms blinked against the dusty light that streamed through the windows.

this small piece of Northern Michigan had not changed

The house was cold and curiously lifeless, its belongings lying inert, a shrine to the warmer days of summer. I felt an intruder, as if our presence were disrupting the normal order of things. The air outside was warmer than in, and we propped open the door to the screen porch so the breeze from the lake could wipe the sleep out of the old structure's eyes. A cobweb fluttered in the corner. A deck of cards sat toppled over on the table, the jack of diamonds exposed. A lone cigarette butt, long cold, rested in a seashell ashtray.

I sat down in a faded, overstuffed chair by the big front windows and pulled a musty quilt over me. Absently, I fingered a copy of the Sunday *New York Times* atop the stack on the floor by the chair. Once so powerful in its original black and white, it now was stiff and yellowed. That the *Times* never made it to the little town near the cottage till two days after publication was something her grandfather loved to tell people when explaining life at the cottage. It was the only place in the world he would tolerate getting his *Times* late, he explained to her as they walked the dusty shoulder into town. Once there, he would fill his old World War I backpack with the paper and as many other things as it would hold, buy her a piece of stick candy when she would rather have had a Three Musketeers, and look in on the gathering of men he joined a few mornings a week for coffee.

On the walk back, she would cradle the paper in her forearms and read aloud. The challenge was to get as much of the front page read as she could before her arms gave out from the sheer weight of the thing. She became a very fast reader, but not fast enough. Her grandfather died before she was old enough to make it through an entire front page.

A fresh breeze leisurely replaced the stale air in the cottage. A flock of gulls danced in and out of the thinning fog, their song, at times, the only hint of their presence. Pulling the quilt around my shoulders, I burrowed a little deeper in the chair, grateful that this small piece of Northern Michigan had not changed.

the hunt club

My first morel hunt didn't begin with a peaceful stroll in a newly green forest. Mine began behind a surging pack of morel zealots, some racing, others managing just a trot as the annual Boyne City Morel Mushroom Festival took to the woods.

My initiation into morel hunting hadn't gone well from the get-go that day. I arrived late, nervous, knowing nothing about finding morels, hoping to get my bearings before the contest began. But as I hurried from my car to join the throng gathered in the field, they were poised to go. And go they did, at great speed or at least as fast as their tennis shoes, battered boots and seldom-tested muscles would take them.

As I ran alongside a heavyset man, he tried to share some information with me, but it was such a struggle for him to talk and jog that I worried for his health and dropped back to catch a woman in a blue windbreaker that promoted an auto repair shop. "Don't focus!" she shouted at me as we ran. "Don't focus!" I felt like David Carradine on "Kung Fu," trying to uncover the wisdom in her words. I cast my lot with her.

Once across the field, she and a small group broke from the pack and headed up a wooded hillside. I followed, never doubting them. And I was beginning to feel the thrill of the hunt. These people knew what they were looking for, and they had the passion to find it. When the group split yet again, as morel-hunting groups are wont to do, I followed the blue windbreaker and found myself shoulder-to-shoulder with a red-haired man and his partner. They were moving slowly, deliberately now, studying the moist ground. They stopped and crouched, a hand up to stop me. I stopped. I crouched. I strained my eyes to pick detail out of last year's leaves, small sprouts of new growth and black earth. The red-haired man inhaled ever so softly. He slowly moved forward as if stalking prey capable of flight. Then his hand shot out. Bingo!

> a small group broke from the pack and headed up the hillside

In the next few minutes he worked a tiny plot of earth and pulled from it a handful of morels, not a one of which I'd seen till they were in his fingers. I whispered my awe and bemoaned my lack of prowess. "You're focusing," he admonished. I glanced at the woman in the windbreaker. Her face seemed strained.

I stayed with the red-haired man till the end of the timed hunt. I looked hopefully at his bag.

"We won't win," he sighed. As we trudged back, I noticed for the first time what a spectacular day it was. The trilliums were popping, and the scent of leeks filled the air. "But how do you do it?" I asked. I hadn't spotted a single morel on my own.

"Ha!" said the red-haired man, "this is nothing. We find garbage bags full of these." End of lesson. Back at the starting line, I chatted my way through the crowd trying to understand what it takes to be, or even want to be, a morel hunter. I surveyed the faces and body language of the winners. I asked questions over kielbasa. But still, as I drove home that night I knew I had not discovered what makes a morel hunter tick.

Seven years later, I married one. We have walked many a woods in the early spring, much of that time separated and apart; me hiking on, marveling at the sights and scents and promise of spring, circling back to find him head down, off the trail, coiled and ready as a grasshopper. And after 10 years of marriage I can identify some salient features of a morel hunter. First is a patient spirit, next, a love of the intricacies of the natural world. And last, there has to be the thrill of the hunt.

If I don't to this day love hunting morels, and I don't, I do love what it does for Neal and our oldest son, Ben. Watching them, I can almost overlook that my husband has used deception, coercion and in one instance, I'm convinced, bribery to find good moreling spots. All is forgiven when my hunters come home streaked with dirt, carrying their bounty and their stories of snakes seen, rabbit holes investigated, gnawed tree trunks examined and bird eggs restored.

When I do hunt morels with my family, I can often be found leaning against a tree trunk, gazing up through the canopy of new leaves, weaving a story for my second son, Peter. As Ben and Neal, with our youngest, Austin, on his back, work the territory surrounding where Peter and I lounge, their earnestness fills the air with such expectation that every now and then I remember the adrenaline rush of dashing up that hillside knowing something elusive was waiting, knowing we would find it.

"Don't focus," I tell Peter as we get to our feet. He always nods solemnly. It's a comfort to know he doesn't get it either.

boundaries

The lawn badly needs mowing. Rain and sun have conspired to produce an acre that needs a machete more than our sputtering, rebuilt Lawn Boy. We had good intentions for this day but woke to our first summer storm: thick sheets of rain, lightning and thunder that seemed to start from somewhere in the center of the Earth. Fierce winds have blown the storm off to the east and left behind a heavy heat that hangs in a fog over the islands. We have decided to wait until tonight to cut the lawn; the grass will have dried in the sun that's come out, and cool evening breezes will wash off the lake.

Our lawn was carved out of a meadow that still runs along two borders; woods butt up against a third. The meadow grass grows tall in a tangled, wild beauty, usually etched in sharp contrast to the clipped green of the lawn. But when our lawn gets this long, the line that divides man and nature begins to blur, reminding that nature quite easily could reclaim this land for its own if it were left alone. But though the blades of grass are venturing into the knee-high field grass and the painted daisies in the garden lean toward the purple iris in the field, neither side seems quite willing to cross the line, to conquer or capitulate.

There was no line to cross in my childhood of tree-lined streets and suburban homes. The smell of a freshly mown lawn evoked well-groomed beauty, an order, safety. On summer nights, I would lie on my back in the damp clippings, searching for stars beyond the glow of porch lights and listening to the predictable sounds of night in the suburbs, the clang of metal as Mr. Kirkpatrick retrieved the trash cans, the occasional bark of a dog asking to be let in or the plaintive cry of "All-y, all-y in come free!" from a few yards over.

the line that divides man and nature begins to blur

But if our newly mown lawn will supply the scent of my protected childhood, the adjacent fields are the look and smell of my childhood dreams. Poplar leaves shimmer in the sunlight, evergreens tower over fields of spent trillium, and sumac have so tangled their limbs that a person cannot pass through. Those fields are a magic world I've been drawn to since I was 10, a land outside the orderly boundaries created by clippers and mowing machines. I was not at all brave about this unpredictability as a child. I was afraid to dangle my toes from my water ski in the middle of the lake for fear of what might bite them. I was nervous as I ran through the woods behind the cottage on my way home at

night, imagining the snipe my brother said lay in waiting. And I lay frozen in my bed watching the moon illuminate a spider's web in the rafters over my bed, home to the insect I most dreaded. I was not brave, but I was entranced. Once introduced to Northern Michigan, the world became a place of infinite mystery, infinite possibility. The sounds were like none I'd heard before. The stars were more glorious than any neon. And the swell of a hillside or massive strength of a 100-year-old hemlock were more captivating than the sight of any skyscraper I'd seen.

I could have chosen to make a life in any of the spectacular places built by man. But I chose instead the sort of beauty and unpredictability that man cannot create. Of course, I know that we've left our mark most everywhere in Northern Michigan. There is a need in some to impose order wherever they imagine there is none, to make predictable beauty to replace that which is not.

Tonight as the smell of fresh-cut grass comes east on the breeze, I'll lie awake and listen to the sounds that are never quite the same night to night. I'll picture the moon casting silver shadows on the deep, dark waters of Lake Michigan, and see in my mind's eye blades of grass forming a carpet of green velvet that wants me to lie down upon it. And I'll conjure the darkened fields and trees that push against the lawn whose mysteries, treacherous and wild, peaceful and serene, exist entirely without me. And as I drift off, I'll quietly ask that we find the strength to not cross every line.

chasing the moon

Tonight there is a full moon. It has been clear and cold, and everyone thought the moon would be brilliant. Instead, a haze of clouds dampens its luster, making its light diffuse and haunting.

Even dimmed, the moon confronts us in spite of ourselves up here, insisting we pay attention to its many permutations like a proud child pulling on our sleeve. It's different in the city, of course, where man-made lights are so bright the moon can't compete. As for the suburbs where I grew up, I don't remember the moon much at all.

The first time I remember being enchanted by the moon I was 11, sitting on the cottage porch late one night with my family. The water glistened under the single moonbeam that sliced the lake in half. My sisters, my brother and I got to musing with my mom about whether it was possible to follow the beam of the moon straight across the lake and what we might find on the other side. If she knew the answer, she didn't tell.

The path down to the dock was lit as if by a spotlight. I remember the rush I felt as we motored the boat straight into that beam. All that was known and ordinary—our hands, our clothes, the trappings of the boat—began to glow in a thrilling and mysterious light. It was a revelation to discover that once you're in a moonbeam it's impossible to determine if you are following it or it is following you. What began as a game of chase became instead a dance. Eventually the purr of the engine and the rich night air put me to sleep. The last thing I remember is my brother at the wheel, his face lit by moonlight and curiosity as we drifted leisurely around the lake.

Years later I watched the same moon from the bed of a friend's pickup. The gentle night breeze smelled of meadow grass. Gray, broken boards of abandoned barns let the moon's light seep through like water, seemingly flooding the barns with light from within. On the flattest roads we turned off the truck's headlights and crept through the county in a strange pact between the manufactured and the natural. The light and the air taken together created a kind of contentment and freedom so that I wanted for absolutely nothing.

all that was known and ordinary began to glow

One night not long ago I woke out of a dead sleep the way parents do when a child hovers near their bed, unsurprised by our five-year-old son, Ben. Our bedroom glowed white from a full moon, making Ben's

67

skin appear the color of aged porcelain, fragile as onionskin. He couldn't sleep; the light was too bright. Clambering into our bed, he exclaimed with glee when he caught a glimpse of the full moon on the lake. As he settled in between us, he asked, almost wistfully, if I remembered when

we had chased the moon up and down the beach. I was taken aback. He couldn't have been older than two the night he'd run along the waterline until he could run no more in a game of cat and mouse with the moon. His laughter had come in peals every time he looked over his shoulder to discover that the moon had followed him. I remembered the night perfectly: his chubby legs, the droplets he kicked up as he ran that hung for an impossible moment in the light around him, the joy I felt, seeing my child so happy. As he recalled his version of that night, I gathered each detail as if I were running behind him with a basket.

I knew, even as I listened to him, that in a year, maybe two, his memory of the night he chased the moon would be gone. That memory will be mine, not his. As will, I'm sure, the memory of us reliving it. Life at two years old, and even five, eventually disappears for all of us. And while so often there is sadness to that truth, I couldn't be sad when it had to do with the moon. I know, as he will someday, that the thrill of being in a moonbeam never really goes away.

when summer's gone

When I was a kid, I dreaded Labor Day. I'd sit at the end of the dock at the cottage and dangle my toes in the still-warm water. The quiet of the lake was somehow sad, and the shoreline lay bare, bereft of its brightly colored boats and flags. I never looked ahead as I sat there. I only looked back—to a summer and a lake that had been filled with shouts and laughter and the purr of small motors. From my perspective, the life of my lake and all of Northern Michigan ended when I left.

I was a young adult before I discovered "the other" Northern Michigan, the one I came to know that first year I stayed on after the arrival of fall. I watched our towns become small again. The cashier at the grocery store had a moment to share a story, and shop owners fired up the coffee pot and chatted as they replenished their stock. I discovered 65-degree afternoons, even some in the 70s, when I found myself the only person on Sturgeon Bay. The lush green forests I knew well became a blaze of reds and golds framed against the kind of blue sky I know now to be September's. Then suddenly, sometimes in one windy weekend, the stark beauty of grays and browns took their place.

Having discovered such contentment and delight in all that comes with fall Up North, I would have thought I'd left my childhood melancholy at summer's end behind. And so, for years, it came as a shock to me when that feeling from the dock of my childhood suddenly resurfaced whenever we passed the quiet of a lake in autumn. I would be caught up by a sense of loss. The placid waters just beginning to mirror fall's grandeur brought a sorrow that even awe could not crowd out.

there's a collective sigh…

This fall, that feeling has been put to rest. After living our first four seasons on a lake I have come to experience summer's end and fall's beginning with relief and anticipation. I understand it means that Northern Michigan's waters, trails and beaches are going to get a well-deserved break, along with the rest of us. There's a collective sigh as we loll all bundled up in the hammock on cool evenings, daydreaming about skiing across the lake for breakfast in town. There are only a few lights around the lake at night now, and nearly all the cottages along our dirt road are shut tight until spring. It's quiet and achingly beautiful.

Just down the road from us, two wooden owls perch nobly on large wooden stumps all summer long, marking the entrance to a neighbors' drive. In the fall, when that older couple heads

south, the owls are put away. Our three-year-old, Ben, is quite taken with these owls; his glee at their arrival early last summer caught me by surprise and seemed to launch the season. One day last month, as Ben pulled his red wagon with all his treasures the half-mile to our mailbox, we stopped and I lifted him up to touch the rough, scarred wood that someone long ago carved into owls. A few days later when we passed, they were gone. Ben was so busy floating the first brightly colored leaves in muddy puddles he didn't make much of their absence. Later, as I was hurrying him home in his soaked sneakers, he gave me the kind of unsolicited take on events that kids often do: the owls had gone somewhere warm because they don't like the snow. "They'll be back," he said simply, eyeing a particularly deep puddle ahead.

Maybe that's one reason why some of us choose to live with four perfectly distinct seasons. The marking of time gives us confidence that no matter what life brings, the leaves will still change color, the snow will fall, first buds will sprout. And one morning, very early, I'll hear the first lonely sound of an outboard, far out on the lake. I'll go down to the dock, dip my toes in the still-cold water and quietly welcome summer's return.

bringing olivia home

It's said that good things come in small packages. Well, our gift this season is the very tiny and brave Olivia (nicknamed Olya, as she was in Russia), the 11-month-old strawberry blond we just brought home from St. Petersburg.

We kissed our three little boys goodbye one morning in September and headed to the airport on the same day a large bomb went off in Moscow. Even now, I wonder how we managed to board that plane. With just two minutes of video and a short medical report on  Olya, it's hard to explain the sense of commitment we felt in spite of the danger. We never hesitated.

Our arrival did little to dispel the images of Communist Russia fed us through decades of Cold War. We made our way through the small, smoky airport, through the stern passport check and customs and then out into the airport's foyer. Due to increased security, the people from our agency were delayed and weren't there to meet us. It was a bit disconcerting.

Pushing our luggage cart outside we came upon another small crowd, looking like the disheartened people standing in lines we'd seen on the news. I put my coat over the plastic-wrapped stroller. We'd been told not to broadcast that we were adoptive parents, as pickpockets would know we were carrying a substantial amount of cash. We waited. Impatient, Neal walked back inside.

The next thing I knew he was calling me over to an unmarked Mercedes, supposedly a cab. Before I could say "Mafia," we were in the back seat of the sedan, sans seat belts, with a Russian we'd never seen before, driving through a bleak landscape marked mostly by cement buildings.

> we all understood how fragile this opportunity was

I needn't have worried. The cab driver turned out to be a delightful man whose only two sons live in America. It was the first of many wonderful, gracious exchanges we had with people. I had the distinct sense that we all understood how fragile this opportunity was.

As we neared the city center, beautiful old buildings began appearing, painted in Mediterranean colors—jade, yellow, salmon and periwinkle. Then came the rivers and canals, the bridges, the archways. We pulled up in front of the Grand Hotel Europe. As we waited in the spectacular lobby, Neal turned to me with a big smile. "So, we're in Russia."

Our eight days were spent moving from sightseeing to endless paperwork to sudden, heart-wrenching moments. Maybe the most poignant came at the end of the long day in which we (along with several other couples) had gone to court and legally adopted the children we had only just met. We were all rather giddy as we drove to the orphanage to actually pick up our kids. It was done. They were now ours to love and raise.

It was already dusk as we pulled into the driveway of the orphanage. We drove slowly past a long row of windows, and suddenly a sea of little toddler faces appeared in the window. We were all stunned, not just because we hadn't known toddlers were at this orphanage, but because those older faces were filled with such awareness and hope. The van got very quiet.

As we turned the corner we came upon about a dozen toddlers in snowsuits playing on some handmade play equipment. Several of them jabbered to us as we got out of the bus. One little one, with a hood pulled so tight we couldn't tell if it was a boy or girl, approached Gordon, one of the dads in our group. He got down on his haunches to try and chat. The child walked right up to him and placed his or her head on Gordon's chest. Gordon put his arms around the child. We all walked into the orphanage in tears and in silence, carrying bags filled with donations and with the new clothes we were going to put on our children. Clothes they would wear as they drove away to new lives.

In the director's office, we took off our coats and waited for the children to be brought to us. I began pulling Olivia's clothes out of the backpack we'd carried everywhere. Reaching for her tiny shoes, I came across the photo album the agency instructed us to put together filled with pictures of family, our home, examples of how we lived. I opened the album. Suddenly, there were the faces of our three little boys, so certain of their place in the world. I touched their faces with my finger. And there, too, was our life in Northern Michigan, a life that is inconceivable to every Russian we had met. I leafed through pictures of us hiking through the national lakeshore, of the boys on cross-country skis as huge snowflakes covered their tracks. There were smiles, so open and trusting as they leapt off the dock holding hands. Confident smiles in such contrast to the quivering, hopeful smiles of the children we'd met in the orphanage.

The director entered, carrying Olya. She noticed the album and we stood side by side, leafing through the pages. She didn't speak English, but smiled enthusiastically as I used the Russian word for "brothers." I only made it through a few pages before I stopped, implying that was the end. I couldn't continue, the contrast was just too overwhelming. The director is a doctor, and we were told she makes $150 a month in a country whose future is very uncertain. She looked up as I closed the album, smiled kindly and stroked Olya's head. Then she left to deliver the other children to their new lives.

I gently laid Olya down and began peeling off the layers of old clothing she wore, down to the loincloth that served as a diaper. She looked up at me with a questioning look and then smiled as her hands reached for the button on my sweater. The clothes I'd brought were way too big, as if they didn't belong to her.

I was alone as I carried her out into the hallway lit only by the gray twilight creeping in from the windows. I held her close. We'd filmed the big wooden playpen with its handful of toys that she knew so well. And we'd filmed the neatly written list on the wall of her room — the names of the babies she shared a room with and their crib numbers. We'd tried to capture all we could. But would I remember to tell her how it felt to walk down that hall, taking her away from the only home she'd ever known, to the life now tucked away in the photo album? Would I remember how the caretaker who passed us smiled so kindly as she said her goodbyes to Olya and then went on down the darkening hall to her work? Would I remember the sound of babies crying?

We got to spend three glorious days getting to know Olya and introducing her to the city of her birth before we caught an evening plane to Moscow. The sun was setting behind us as we walked across the tarmac. I tried to shelter her from the wind blowing across the airfield. But as is her nature, she put her head up on my shoulder to face the wind head on and watch the world around her. I whispered to her about where we were going and about what she was leaving behind. I daydreamed out loud about the times we would return, her brothers in tow. She was making motorboat sounds. I was crying.

I looked back to see what would be her last vision of the country of her birth. She was looking up at a cloud drenched in the last brilliant light of the sunset. We stepped into the plane.

waxing gibbous

Out our bedroom window, the wind off Lake Michigan is gathering force, rushing through the barren branches of winter trees in a race with itself. Occasionally there are half-hearted spits of snow. The horizon, pale gray, shows no sign of the storm that is brewing. The sky is calm, a mask; a game it likes to play. The two feet of snow we've had lies under a solid crust of ice over which small branches and leaves career like out-of-control skaters.

We are to have a storm. That's all right. The wood box is full. The dog's wheezing signals a deep sleep. The house is warm and safe, creaking gently.

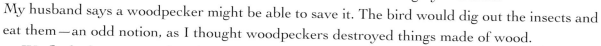

I dreamed last night that a pileated woodpecker came to the hunk of suet that hangs from the massive, old maple across the yard. But this morning there were only overstuffed blue jays, gorging themselves on the fat. The tree is dying, slowly being eaten by some unseen insect. One side of its trunk is stripped of bark and lies pocked and exposed. Three of its most noble branches are gray and dead. My husband says a woodpecker might be able to save it. The bird would dig out the insects and eat them—an odd notion, as I thought woodpeckers destroyed things made of wood.

We flushed a grouse a few days ago, just after we'd flown down a winding trail on our skis. As we climbed slowly past the spot where the bird had taken flight, we saw a small hole dug through the snow to the earth. Bits of wood, earth and shell were littered about the mouth. When we got home, Neal read to figure out if there was a connection between the hole and the grouse.

"A large red-brown or gray-brown chickenlike bird of brushy woodlands, usually not seen until it flushes with a startling whirl." No mention of holes in the snow. He read on: "Drumming of male suggests a distant motor starting up. The muffled thumping starts slowly, accelerating into a whir." He stopped reading. We stared at each other in amazement. We were both remembering the day last year as we walked lazily through a spring-green forest. He had stopped in his tracks when he heard it: a low rumbling that for years I had thought to be either my own heart or the sound of a tractor turning over, miles away. Neither of us had known what it was, but I took comfort in knowing he had heard it, too. It was the drumming of a grouse. What incredible power that small bird must possess in its wings.

There will be a full moon tonight, but I doubt the storm will let us see it. Last weekend the moon was a waxing gibbous, and it shone brilliantly through the clearest of winter skies. "Waxing gibbous" is a new term for me. As are "waning gibbous" and "waxing crescent." I knew that a waxing moon is one on the way to full, and that waning indicates it's on its way back down. But I'd never heard the term "gibbous" until after dinner one night when Tom Babel, a world-class sailor, explained that "gibbous" means anything between a half and a full moon, while crescent refers to any moon that is smaller than half.

All good and well, I thought later that night as his wife, Janet, and I stood staring at a three-quarter moon, but how do you know which way it is headed? "Left side lit last," offered Janet. If the left side has yet to be lit, the moon is waxing. If only the left side is lit, the moon is waning.

My relationship with the land and water and skies of Northern Michigan has always been a soulful thing, a thing of the heart. Discovering the intricate rhythms and rules of nature is not unlike the challenge and intrigue of learning about a complicated friend. If you're lucky, knowledge breeds respect. If you're lucky, the friendship only grows stronger.

shred betty gets a lesson

It's hard to believe now, after so many picture-perfect early spring days, that we were ever unhappy about El Niño. But, last winter, we cursed El Niño, supposedly the cause of the season's warm weather and meager snowfall. We blamed it for everything from a sluggish economy to marital strife to weight gain, and as I sat watching the whiz-bang cast hardening on my arm last February, I didn't blame myself for my situation, I blamed El Niño.

Last February, before El Niño really kicked in, Neal and I were anticipating a couple of days without children. Our working title for those days was "Things you never get to do because you're with the kids." Sleeping past 6:30 a.m., lingering over coffee at a café and actually reading a newspaper, browsing in the bookstore through books with more than 12 words on a page. And lots of cross-country skiing. We wanted the beauty, the tranquility and the aerobic workout of cross-country skiing, followed by food and drink with no witching hour.

> I couldn't even make it up the towrope

Then the snow began to melt. El Niño left bare patches of dirt in the woods and on the trails. There would be no cross-country skiing. At loose ends on our second day, we decided on downhill skiing where weeks' worth of snowmaking still provided a base.

We'd been skiing into the late morning when on one chairlift ride we acknowledged that skiing that day just wasn't fitting the bill; we needed an adventure. Suddenly, there it was, right below us. Snowboarding—an impulse I'd never had before. And yes, I'd cursed once as I shepherded my little ones through the melee of shredders. But all that was forgiven, displaced by the prospect of doing something truly new.

We laughed our way through the rental process. Did we want our left foot forward or our right? Oh, who knows, why not the left! We ignored the neon sign in our heads flashing three simple words, "Take a lesson!" As we tucked the boards under our arms ready to head out, one guy sobered a bit. You might want to think about a lesson, he suggested. How hard can it be, we exclaimed. He shook his head. In a snap we were on the slopes.

I'm one of those lucky people who learned a lot of recreational things as a child, which gives me a frame of reference for most activities. Not snowboarding. I couldn't even make it up the towrope. When I fell they stopped the tow, leaving me to the silent contempt of the six-year-old behind me as I crawled away from the rope.

Neal made it to the top on his first try. As I sat resting from my crawl, I caught sight of him careening away from the tow at the top. He gained his composure and was looking pretty good, and that was the last I saw of him. He hadn't a clue about turning so he traversed himself right off the bunny hill and down its steeper side, joining an intermediate run. I think it was him I heard screaming, but couldn't be sure; there's a lot of that on the bunny hill.

Left on my own, I stood up, got my free foot in place and immediately the board was in motion. I had no control whatsoever. After all my years of skiing, waterskiing, sledding, I could find no frame of reference for how to turn, stop, do anything but veer headlong into a four-year-old and her mother. I registered their look of horror as I threw myself to the ground inches from their ski tips. I apologized, wincing; my sacrum had taken a blow.

It wasn't the last fall of the day. I fell relentlessly. Neal reappeared, undamaged, and over the next hour or two he began to master key moves. It's kind of like skateboarding, he would call out to me as he flew by. As if that would help; it was the one sport I had missed as a kid. And yet, watching him, I was sort of getting the hang of it.

At some point, I abandoned the towrope, no longer able to absorb the disdain of preschoolers or welcome the earnest suggestion from the young operator that I take a lesson. On my last run from the spot halfway up the bunny hill that had become my launching pad, I felt myself falling yet again. Knowing my sacrum just couldn't take another hit, I put my hands behind me to break my fall. My right arm took the lion's share of the fall, and I knew immediately: it was hurt. Still, my spirits remained high. The sun was just settling on the top of the hills, it had been a beautiful day and a good meal awaited us. Besides, it's not like I would break a bone.

A painful week later, I decided it might be time for an X-ray. Broken. As the orthopedist wrapped the cast on my arm, he talked about the impact of snowboarding on his practice. With skiers, he gets broken legs, but snowboarders present wrists, arms, even a few shoulders. His advice was, it's a great sport, but take a lesson. That had a familiar ring.

Wearing a cast got very old, very quickly. It was a kick to see the faces of my son's seven-year-old buddies when they heard I'd busted my arm snowboarding. For a few minutes, I was back in third grade, awed by Billy Conn's full leg cast. Ahh, I thought, every time I attempted to zip my sons' coats, what a luxury to break bones when you still have your mother around.

Will I ever be a "shred Betty" again? Maybe, but I'll take a lesson. What worries me more is what will happen the next time those warm El Niño days and blue skies send us looking for adventure. I so hope it's not skydiving.

rural route

Our mailbox is at the end of our dirt road, a half-mile from the house. We gave this nary a thought when we moved our family—two-and-a-half-year-old Ben, one-week-old Peter and our aging dog Sara—into our little spot on the lake. But we'd never lived with a mailbox farther away than the end of our drive, and we quickly found the distance disconcerting. We added coordinating which of us would get the mail to our hectic daily schedule, lest we discover we'd forgotten it just as we settled in for a winter evening. On occasion we'd forget anyway. Sometimes we'd leave it until the next day, but that was surprisingly hard to do.

As we got settled and Peter grew heartier, I took to bundling the boys onto the sled for a trip up the plowed road to get the mail. In any season, it's a beautiful walk. What houses there are sit tucked behind curtains of cedar and poplar. Three streams flow under the road, reappearing like magic on the other side, and animal tracks abound.

We'd usually set off on our outing in high spirits, Ben marching along in his tri-colored snow boots, Sara making half-hearted attempts to follow a rabbit scent. If we were lucky, Peter would doze.

But a mile roundtrip was about a half-mile too long for the baby when traveling at the pace of a snow-suited toddler. Soon after we'd turn for home, Peter no longer would be dozing or cooing or even whimpering. He'd be screaming. Opting for speed, I'd load Ben back into the sled against his will. To keep him from crying as well, I'd give him the mail to carry. We'd no sooner get going than Sara would turn her wise, tired eyes to me, sit down and not move. "Just let me catch my breath a minute," she would have said if she could. The baby crying, my poor old dog resting and Ben "reading" and then dispensing Newsweek and the phone bill into the slush and snow; it was no longer the walk down the lane I hoped for.

Our standard-issue mailbox still stands as a sentry marking the end of what our four kids call our "bumpy" road and the beginning of the paved, county road. And through sun, rain, sleet and snow we've made our way to the mail on foot, skis, snowshoes, bikes and wagons. Over the years, the boys have discovered brilliant green frogs in the streams, floated boats and soaked countless numbers of shoes and boots in the chilly water. They've learned which wildflowers come up when and blown the white fluff out of hundreds of cattails. Tadpole catchers, butterfly nets and worm homes have hastily been built to take with us on the trek.

Sometimes our walks are raucous fun, and the trip goes in a wink. Sometimes it seems to take forever, when they're fighting over who gets to carry the mail or whining that they just can't make it without food or water. And sometimes, unpredictably, at noon or dusk, they are quiet, reflective, content to hang close and share a story or a secret or maybe just the sound of the wind in the trees.

The trip to the box has always required an adult—until this summer when, for the first time, the kids started going on their own. A few times a week, a ragtag group of siblings and friends set off to get the mail, walking our new dog, Foxy.

it never
occurred to
me to
worry about
the mail

I was hesitant the first time I let them head off, reviewing carefully the procedure for crossing the "busy" road. They run unescorted up and down the dirt road all they like, but crossing the paved road to the mailbox with summer traffic buzzing past was a worry.

As they ran up the drive that first time, I could still see them as toddlers bustling up the hill on sturdy legs. And I could still feel Sara bumping up against my leg every now and then so I'd stop walking and crouch down to give her a rest and a scratch between her ears. As I walked back toward the house, I looked to the cedar grove by way of a hello to Sara, my old companion who'd been buried there five years before. Then I settled in a chair on the porch to wait for the adventurers' return, conscious of the still quiet that had been left in their wake.

In relatively short order, back they came—running down the driveway with such abandon it seemed their legs had gotten away from their bodies. Foxy, a herder, gleefully worked the edges of the group to keep them bunched together. With faces hot and flushed they stormed my perch, thrusting pieces of mail in my direction out of sticky hands that are still so small. Then, just as quickly, they were off to the lake.

One day, a neighbor knocked on the door, a clump of soggy envelopes in her hand. She found the random collection of bills and special offers in the woods along the road when looking for her lost cat. They were ours, of course. Funny, I thought, as I peeled the wet paper apart, in all the time I spent worrying about the kids, it never occurred to me to worry about the mail.

Last week, they actually convinced me to let them take their 21-month-old sister Olivia along—only as far as the last bend in the dirt road so she wouldn't be near the traffic. She was beside herself with joy and sat perched in her stroller, ready for anything. Of course, Olivia being Olivia, she refused to stay in her stroller, wanted to swim in the brooks and wander into the marshy swamps of the forest. Needless to say, her trips to the mailbox will be with me along for a few more years. And for a while longer, so will lots of theirs.

And that suits me just fine.

summer of '67

It was our Camelot, a place in time where everything good seemed magnified. The smiles were bigger, the beds cozier, the skies bluer than we'd ever seen. It was the summer of 1967.

I was the youngest in a family that stood on the threshold of change. Not only were we growing up, the world itself was changing, certainly our world at home in Detroit. But there was magic in the air of Northern Michigan, and the days that summer were measured in daydreams and adventures. Our paths were lit by laughter and it seemed I was always following the sound of it. I would chase it down the tree-lined steps that led to the water, my heart racing as I heard the squeals coming from the swimming raft just as my brother plunged into the water, relinquishing his throne as king of the mountain. Laughter would draw me up the steps to the attic room I shared with my two sisters, where Pam and Wendy lounged on the double beds in sleeveless blouses and plaid Bermudas, sharing some delightful secret in the dusty sunlight. And laughter would float out to the porch at night from the room inside where my parents sat, finding me as I lay reading under a light that glowed deep yellow from a faded lampshade. My parents' laughter joined the trail of smoke from my father's cigarette, and danced and twined toward the screen, seeping slowly out into the darkness.

Most nights we played cards around an old wooden table, sometimes locked in mortal combat but more often caught up in raucous laughter. One year the obsession was hearts. The next my mom taught us pinochle. But the game that prevailed through the years was a game called "Oh, Hell." It was a nail-biter for those among us who liked to go for broke. My mom and I didn't; my brother did. We knew each other very well when it came to cards. It seemed we knew each other well, period.

Into our summer idyll came a rite of passage: My oldest sister got her driver's license. We all went, squirming in anticipation on our drive to the county seat. The first of us was getting wings. Wearing the only "school clothes" she'd brought to the cottage, her signature pin at her collar, Pam told my mother how desperately she hoped she could parallel park when the time came. We, of course, desperately hoped she could, too.

we knew
each other
well when
it came
to cards

We needn't have worried. The man who tested her was far more interested in the car, a gold Olds '98 convertible with its black top down, than in my sister's driving abilities. And when my mother used the smile she usually reserved for the produce man at Kroger's, Pam was a shoe-in. But even my mom was surprised when they returned from the test in less than three minutes. "No parallel parking," Pam whispered to my sister Wendy, and the rest of us immediately vowed we'd come North for our driving tests.

I knew somehow that more change was to come, and I was glad to be far from home, in a place where time seemed to pass more slowly. At night, especially on Fridays after my father had arrived, I would lie in my bed listening to the sound of the crickets over my sisters' soft breathing as they slept, and I would wish that I could keep us all there together, but I couldn't. We grew up, left home, and each in my family carried that memory of Up North with them through every sort of change, to all parts of the country and different parts of the world. And now we have all come back, seeking again the smells, the sounds, the pace and the beauty of life here. We returned in search of each other. From far off, we followed the sound of our own laughter and found it waiting.

november

It wasn't until I hit the clearing that I realized I was walking into a storm. Magnificent, low-hanging clouds formed a solid shelf over Lake Michigan, the far side of which was a gorgeous green-blue sky. A screen of black rain spilled into the lake several miles out. The sky above me was an odd yellow-gray.

The dog hung at my knee, ears flat to her head, while slowly the world around us went dark. The wind began to howl so that I could no longer hear my breath. The deep red of the sumac and coal-black trunks of the poplars fell into shadow.

I heard it before I felt it. Hail. Perfectly formed, tiny balls of ice, bouncing off my rain jacket and scurrying along the pavement like a million marbles let loose down a hill. I felt the clouds part and looked up quickly enough to see the sun force itself through the edge of one bursting gray cumulonimbus. It seemed I was looking into heaven. And through it all, the almost gentle barrage of hail continued. It was powerful, exhilarating, completely, uncontrollably wonderful. November was everywhere.

November seems a month for poetry. It promises windy, gray, reflective days, powerful skies and ghostlike horizons. Time rests on your shoulders like a gift bestowed between more brilliant months whose offerings demand activity. While some people find November a month to be wary of, I find it a particularly honest month. Honest and raw. Even as it twists and turns, it wears no illusions. The perils it so regularly presents are neither hidden nor unexpected. And in the face of them, there is a time that is right for questions, speculations. November days encourage you to cultivate daydreams, or share those of another.

time rests
on your
shoulders
like a gift

I lit the stove for the first time this season on an afternoon when sleet flung itself headlong against the windows. The wood took quickly and the smell of it burning was poignant as a childhood memory. It brought with it a sense of preparedness, security against the impending weather of winter. And as the wind whistled to the trees and the windows strained just slightly, I poured myself a cup of coffee, put up my feet and gave myself over to my imaginings. November had arrived.

colonel mustard in the morning

6:15 a.m. Olivia has been up for a half-hour and her chattering has awakened our three boys. They wander down to curl up on the couch, bleary-eyed, hair rumpled, still in the long johns they wore skiing the night before. It is black as night outside and the coffee is just now ready.

By 6:25, Austin, 3, has drifted to the Legos, Peter, 6, is struggling to get into his knight-in-shining-armor costume and Ben, 8, has happened on Monopoly. I groan.

As a child, one of the parts of life at the cottage I loved most was time spent as a family playing cards and board games. Once back home, there never seemed to be time. As the youngest, I felt keenly the loss of that time together. Thus, my vow—if I ever had a family, we would play games at home, often, not just when thrown together on vacation. And now, here I am, confronted with Monopoly before the sun is up.

The game is out of the chest and on its way to the kitchen table with the boys before I can mumble to Neal, "I can't do Monopoly this early in the morning. It will go on and on. It has no end."

Hastily, Neal and I decide that I should get the Clue game out of the closet where I've been keeping it for just such an occasion. The boys groan as they look up from their ocean of brightly colored Monopoly money.

This is going to be a tough sell. I pull out all the stops. "It's about someone getting murdered, and you have to figure out who did it and what weapon they used." The boys are stunned. Silence gives way to complete elation.

"Someone gets murdered!"

"There are weapons!"

Neal takes the instructions and begins reading. Hmmm, an uncommon experience. I put Olivia in her high chair with some bananas. It's decided I will team up with Peter, and Neal and Austin will be a team. Ben is on his own.

Neal introduces the victim, a Mr. Bogey. In all the years I've played Clue I never heard the name of the victim.

"Where's Mr. Bogey?" asks Peter. "I want to see him."

"You can't," says Austin. "He got taken down there and got buried. Probably in sand. Probably head first." Peter scours the board.

Neal reads that it doesn't matter if some players receive more cards than others. He looks up at me. "They obviously don't know our family."

"Mom!" says Ben, holding up the tiny, silver candlestick. "This candlestick is a weapon. How?"

"The murderer uses it to bludgeon his victim." They stare at me. All right, I'm talking bludgeoning with my children before the sun is up, but at least I've introduced a new word. I reach for my coffee.

"No," says Austin, "that's not how. You light the candle and set someone on fire with it." Candyland is looking pretty darn good about now.

"Is this game scary?" asks Peter. "The house looks spooky. Do we get murdered like Mr. Bogey? Where is Mr. Bogey?"

Olivia has begun to smear her bananas around her high chair tray.

"Okay," says Neal, "Miss Scarlet always goes first."

"I'm Miss Scarlet!" all three boys call out.

Olivia has had it with the bananas. I get her out of her high chair and clean her up. She's off.

"See that arrow pointing down? That's where Mr. Bogey is shoveled under the sand," says Peter. "I think we should dig him up."

"He's dead, Peter," says Ben.

"Bludgeoned," confirms Austin. Peter looks near tears.

We all have our cards. Austin leaps forward. "Daddy! Look! We got a weapon! It's a … it's a … stick." Ben and Peter are oblivious. They don't know about lead pipes.

"Mom," says Ben, "Olivia's eating a refrigerator magnet."

I retrieve the magnet and have Peter suggest that the crime was committed in the ballroom by Mrs. Peacock with a wrench.

"If you're wondering how you murder someone with a rope," says Austin, "you wrap it around their neck and pull really, really hard and their eyes pop out and they can't see and they fall down and die."

I decide it's better to ignore him.

"Is anyone listening to me?" he asks.

Neal decides to take the secret passage from the kitchen to the conservatory. Austin leaps to his feet. "What's in the secret passage?" he asks. "Is it under the house? I don't think we should take it!"

"Maybe you'll see Mr. Bogey," offers Peter.

Neal moves to the conservatory with a giant leap in the air. Austin now thinks Professor Plum can fly. That's trouble.

"Remember when Daddy was reading the directions?" asks Peter. "That was boring."

"What if I marked the wrong one?" asks Ben, looking very worried.

"What did I have for breakfast?" asks Austin.

I suggest that Professor Plum murdered Mr. Bogey in the library with a knife. Ben proves me wrong. Peter makes a great show of covering the checklist and trying to read the word "knife." He can't find it.

"It's a magic 'e' word," says Ben. I see Peter mark rope.

"Who has the card with the gun?" asks Austin.

"The revolver," says Ben, rolling his eyes.

"It's a gun to me," says Austin.

"Olivia's got the telephone!"

"Who owns this game?"

Neal suggests it was Professor Plum in the ballroom with the wrench. We can't prove him wrong. They check the envelope. And, yes, they are right.

"Oh, I was sure it was Mrs. Peacock because she looks so mean on this card," says Ben. "Just like Cruella DeVille. I just kept making sure I didn't end up in a room with her."

"Mom, I almost got all the skin back from my big bleeding thumb," says Austin.

"Let's play again," says Ben.

"Who do we murder this time?" asks Peter.

"Mr. Bogey," Neal replies.

"He's already dead," says Peter.

"We just pretend to murder him again and again," says Neal.

"Does his family know this?" asks Peter.

"I don't want to murder Mr. Bogey again," says Austin. "Let's let him go home."

"Can we just play?" mumbles Ben.

Olivia enters wearing a cowboy hat and yellow rubber rain boots. The just-rising sun is turning the snow on the lake the softest hint of lavender. There's half a pot of coffee left. And I've got a good feeling about Colonel Mustard.

crossing country

There is a blizzard outside my office window, our first of the season, and all I can think about is getting home to ski. I've finally gotten myself to where I've wanted to be since I was a kid—I can ski out my back door. This is my first winter in the house I bought last spring, around which the Sleeping Bear Dunes National Lakeshore stretches for miles, acres and acres of which I have still to explore.

When I used to picture skiing out my back door, it was modeled on images I had of Scandinavians who commuted on skis. But I'd never heard of Nordic skiing, so I imagined them all lumbering about on downhill skis. So taken was I with this idea that, at age nine or so, I wrote pages and pages of a book about a village in Norway equipped with an elaborate system of tow ropes so people could get back to their homes from the grocery store. There were even tows on the flats to make skiing without the help of gravity less exhausting.

But that imaginary mountain village had plenty of downhill runs, and oh, did I love going downhill. And fast. I started skiing pretty young, thanks to my dad, and I was fearless; no hill was too steep, no mogul too large. Mornings were spent flying off handmade ski jumps with my siblings and friends or winding through the woods on the narrow trails we carved out. The afternoons were for skiing with my dad. I would follow him down any hill he chose, which, given his skills, were the most challenging. He would be a picture of pure technique, curving gracefully about halfway down the hill when I would push off from the top. Straight down; no turns, not a one. Braids flew behind me like telltales in a strong wind, no poles, in a crouch. My style wasn't built for looks. My eyes would water despite my goggles, and my legs would vibrate with the slapping of my skis. Sometimes I would fall on the way down and roll over and over in what my mother would have called a terrifying, head-long tumble. I was never hurt. I would brush myself off, laughing about the fall with my dad as we rode back up on the chairlift. It was just the two of us, legs swinging gently off the chair. I liked that.

my style wasn't built for looks

Then, at about age 11, I suddenly got interested in learning to ski—the right way. My dad says it was when I began to know fear. All the adult concerns that come with trying to control the process came to the fore, crowding out the exhilaration of reckless abandon I'd always known. For the first time, I understood risk. As younger kids flew past me—straight down, in a crouch—just as I'd painstakingly completed a stem Christie, I was annoyed, angry, but a bit wistful. I hated feeling hesitant on the face of a steep run, or creeping around the edge of a mogul. I got very serious. I even began caring about my outfit. And with my dad as my guide, I became a graceful downhill skier. It had its own rewards, but pure, unadulterated joy was not one of them.

I was a sophomore in college when I first saw cross-country skis. Imagine my delight as I instantly transformed my Nordic village from a noisy world of pulleys and machines into a serene, snow-white wonderland. As for reality, I didn't take to Nordic skiing right away. Its charms eluded me. I was not fond of flat surfaces and, having mastered control on a downhill run, careening headlong down a tiny path through trees without my heels locked to the boards, seemed close to suicidal. But if I wanted to be out in the winter, I knew I had to learn; I could only muster the money for a weekend, maybe two, of downhilling.

It didn't take long before I was hooked. I was struck first by the freedom of cross-country; just strap on your skis and go, no nook or cranny is out of the question. And no day is too cold. The fluid, graceful, constant motion is a natural insulator. I love the peace on snowy afternoons, gliding silently through stands of birch, listening to nothing but the steady whoosh of your skis and the pounding of your heart. And I have spent many a blue-sky day, when the sun burns almost white, climbing with friends to perches I never knew existed, the land and water stretching below us in sparse, glistening beauty.

But I love something else about cross-country skiing. I love the risk. Sometimes I stand at the top of a hill peering down a path that winds precariously through a row of evergreens like the dashing of a wild river, and I think about what could happen—disfigurement or worse. I feel my heart start to pump and my breath come in faster gulps. I think about the two thin skis that are controlled only by the pressure I can exert from the balls of my feet. I push off and fly down the path. My eyes water, my cheeks burn, my legs vibrate with the flutter of my skis, and I'm eight years old again, all grown up.

safekeeping

In Detroit on business, in a funny mood and with a little time on my hands, I went to the church I attended so many years ago, from infancy until I left for college. I walked the grounds, which lie at the edge of a little lake, stood alone in the nave, went to the small chapel where the children had Sunday services all their own. Growing up, church and the dinner table were the places my family was together, all six of us. As I wandered, I wasn't surprised to see the church virtually unchanged, but I was surprised how pleased that made me. Not just because a piece of my past was intact, but also because the church is still intact for those who have come after us.

I drove back North on a day defined by color: red and orange and black against patches of blue. North of West Branch, the sun filtered through storm clouds the color of stone. The news on the radio was about a sniper in Virginia and Maryland and the possibility of war in Iraq. When I came in the door of our house, a shower of homemade confetti came down on my head, accompanied by great whoops from my children.

That night, I lay with my daughter as she went off to sleep and then went into the three boys' room. There were questions about my trip, permission slips to be signed, pressing concerns about lost toys. Eventually I picked up the book we're reading but before I settled in, I stopped to look at the moon in the window over my oldest son's head. In that moment of quiet I wanted to tell them about what it means in this world to be able to watch your children fall asleep safely, bathed in moonlight. I thought about telling them how I'd seen my old church so unchanged and about how it felt to drive home knowing that with each mile I was closer to the woods and water that have been my sanctuary all my adult life. But I had no real hope of making myself understood and didn't want to puzzle them.

their
playgrounds
are
hallowed
places

Someday, I do want to find the words and the ways to let my children know that the hills and beaches, the dunes and fields and orchards that are now their playgrounds are hallowed places. Places that deserve to be cherished and preserved as one would protect a 100-year-old church—for themselves, for their children and for all those who will come after. I want to help them understand that those landscapes they roam are not just for the taking—that there exists a great and demanding responsibility to participate in preserving them.

But for them, as for many of us adults, it's much easier to sign on when things are concrete. That's why Neal and I will begin preserving land in our children's names this year—272 square feet for each of them, $30 apiece. It will be a Christmas present and they will get a gift card from the Leelanau Conservancy that says so. They will get certificates over the years, keeping track of their accumulating acreage, making real the impact of our participation and their sacrifice of a toy or two at Christmas or on birthdays. And I'm going to encourage them to give land, little pieces of it, with money from their own bank accounts, so they can combine the pleasure of giving with the beginnings of understanding what stewardship means.

We'll do those things and more as time goes on. But that night of my return, I just turned on the lamp and began to read, stopping occasionally to gaze at the moon and to listen as each of them left my voice behind and drifted off to sleep.

This holiday season, in the new year and in all the years to come, I wish for you a place of peace, wherever that may be. And if that place is out-of-doors in Northern Michigan, I hope my family and I have done our very best to preserve that which we love, for you and for those yet to come.

seeing spring

It was dinner table chatter, one child posing the question, "Which do you like better, winter or summer?" As the other kids pondered their answers, I asked why spring and fall were not included. Quizzical expressions, bony-shouldered shrugs: No one considered my question worth commenting on.

Is an appreciation of spring a function of age, I wondered? Certainly we all remember throwing open school doors on the first warm day, coats trailing behind us like so much dead weight. Were we exulting in the arrival of spring? Or skipping over it, thinking only that summer now must be just around the corner?

While the merits of snowboarding versus tubing on the lake were debated, my mind drifted through springs past, searching for when I first might have appreciated what the coming of spring means, not as a tonic for what preceded it or a harbinger of what was to come, but for itself.

My first vision of a spring came easily to mind, a result, I suspect, of how memories involving several senses are easier to summon. I was recalling a walk I took behind my oldest sister's Northern Michigan farmhouse when I was visiting from college. The night before, I'd sat under a streetlight on the campus curb with my bag, watching for the car that would take me North with my brother and a few of his friends coming from Chicago. Squeezing into the backseat, I felt as if they'd come stealthily, in darkness, to snip barbed wire and spring me from all that seemed at that moment both tedious and overwhelming. As we left my college, there must have been leaves on the trees.

Early the next morning, after several cups of my sister's strong coffee and the eggs she cooked on a wood cookstove, I headed up a trail out her back door. The trail wound through the woods, up a hill and into an opening at the top, from which you could survey Lake Michigan and the islands in the distance, sometimes crystal-clear, sometimes shrouded like ghost ships. As I climbed, I had a goal, a spot with a tree to lean against to watch the sun on the water and think, or not think, as was my wont.

But I wasn't long in the woods before I was stopped short, caught by the kind of beauty that hurts because it is so hopeful, so alive, so unreachable and yet right there. Tiny, brilliant green

leaves sprouted from pencil-thin stems on black branches, seeming to defy physics as the persistent breeze tossed them about, shimmering in the sunlight. My footsteps left impressions in the pungent earth, and I looked back as they filled in my wake, as if I'd never walked that path. All around me birds, well into their day, bustled about with the urgency that spring requires of them, and yet their singing never ceased.

It was an hour before I began to climb again, caught up in a reverie that still came easily at that age, although I would not have said so then. I was burdened with my studies and the weighty questions of the day, forgetting for too long how easily beauty could surprise. As I made my way to the top of the hill, I understood in some way that those woods in springtime had lifted my spirits, lightened my load.

Ten years later, on a chilled blustery day in early April, I bought my first house Up North. I was 30 years old, owner of a still-struggling business, keeper of a dream that had invigorated my life and at the same time, aged me. A relationship that had lasted for much of my 20s had ended, and I was the better for it being over, as was he. But facing a new decade with neither professional success nor marriage and family, I was casting about for permanence. And thus I begged my way into a land contract for a green farmhouse, a mile's walk from Lake Michigan, surrounded by hardwood forests, fields of sumac, towering hemlocks. The payment was $413.89 a month, and as I walked out of the Realtor's office I told myself: if I can find a way to make that payment I will have a home. Forever.

Then panic set in. What had I done? I had taken on the burden of a house, alone, on top of too many other responsibilities. I'd only been in the house twice in my life. My palms sweat as I lay awake at night. A few weeks later the Realtor called to say that the family living in the house was away for the weekend but would be moving out the following week, and I could move in. By this time, I'd begun to view the house as the centerpiece of a horror movie. To regain a bit of sanity, I drove out to the house that Saturday to see if I could remind myself of what I'd seen in the place before I stepped off the cliff.

Once there, I sat on the front porch. A row of brilliant yellow daffodils danced in and about the hemlocks that lined the front yard. The world was silent as I turned my face to the first warm sun of spring and breathed in air that smelled of wild lilacs. I walked round the yard where small patches of crocuses popped through the grass, then wove my way through the sumac as I began to climb the hill behind the house. I was breathing hard when I got to the top and turned to see what I could see.

What I saw took my breath. Before me, crisp as a postcard photo, was Lake Michigan, the powerful face of the dune at Pyramid Point, South Manitou Island and below me, my new home. I stayed up there until the breeze got cold and pushed me to my feet. My footsteps left impressions in the still spongy earth, and if I'd have looked back, I would have realized they disappeared as quickly as I'd made them.

But it was the first real day of spring. And I wasn't looking back.

a ticket to ride

At one time, I imagine her to have been a stunning red. Her freshly varnished seats and oars must have glistened copper brown and her oarlocks shone silver. But by the time I saw her, shoved unceremoniously under some shrubs on the beach, her glory had faded. She was nothing more than a castaway rowboat; peeling paint carpeted the sand around her, seats guaranteed only splinters. No one else in my world gave her a thought, and that was my good fortune.

My older brother and sisters were far too smitten with our powerful inboard to be concerned with a broken-down rowboat. Granted, given the choice between captaining the powerboat or the rowboat, I'd have gone for the bigger, faster, newer. But there was a line of captains ahead of me. If I was allowed on the big boat at all it was only as a passenger, and I was regularly the first booted off if there was a crowd. It was the rowboat, scruffy and small, that would be my ticket to adventure.

In it I explored crevices of the shoreline or bobbed about in the center of the lake lazily imagining what sorts of man-eating fish lurked in the black waters below. I rowed all the way to the little village in search of forbidden Lik-m-aid candy, which I would devour in its entirety on the way home, leaving the oars sticky and my mouth stained a telltale green or orange that not even a swim would fade.

Of course, it took me forever to get anywhere; the boat was wide and heavy and my arms would ache as I struggled home through the saturated colors of a late afternoon. But I never really cared. In fact, I never took much notice of the effort involved at all until our neighbors went home and left us their 10-horsepower engine. It was decided that the motor should be mounted on the old rowboat. At first I balked. Not only did I not want the added weight, I knew that the motor would make her a good deal more attractive to the others.

I was still balking as my brother made me pull the cord again and again, insisting that I learn to start the motor myself. It started finally, suddenly, with a roar and a kick that knocked my knees out from under me and sat me down hard on the seat. There was only time for a panicked glance back toward my brother as he yelled instructions from the beach.

But then, there I was, flying across the lake, and I knew my rowing days were over. Suddenly the sky was the limit, the world a place of boundless opportunity. And I was sure my faded, red rowboat felt just the same way.

october 31st in the country

The headlights sprang from the dark at the end of the gravel drive to my farmhouse. I stretched to see who it was just as the dome light in the truck revealed a young boy dressed as Batman scrambling out the passenger door. In a panic, I ran for the kitchen.

This was my second Halloween in the country. I'd cut my trick-or-treat teeth on a couple of Halloweens in the city where candy vanished by the handful into the pails and pillowcases that swept through my neighborhood like locusts through Egypt. So I'd had lots and lots of candy my first year in the farmhouse as I waited for the country kids to appear. Not a single trick-or-treater came to my door.

And then, a year later, here's this skinny towhead holding open his plastic grocery bag with that look of expectation. Apologetically, I dropped in a box of raisins and a granola bar, the only things I'd been able to scrounge in my frantic search of the cupboards. His eyes followed my treats into his nearly empty bag with a look of confusion; they lay there like alien things, horrifying us both. Twenty years ago now, and the last time I was unprepared, but that little boy was my one and only trick-or-treater in the six years I lived on that rural road. I didn't have a clue where country kids trick-or-treated, but it was clear they weren't roaming from house to house in the countryside.

Now I've ended up with four country trick-or-treaters of my own. For years, when the oldest were small, we'd drive around to a few friends' houses, returning home with five or six pieces of candy, a caramel apple and, always, a specially decorated cupcake. As they got older, we headed for the village that includes their school, their church, the small grocery store where they

not a single trick-or-treater came to my door

sometimes get after-school snacks. There are few sidewalks. Streetlights dangle over only a few intersections. For long stretches we walk with friends in the dark, the porch lights never reaching all the way to the road. Many houses are dark as well, their owners south now. We drink coffee that steams in the nippy air and call endlessly to the small, shadowy figures that dart ahead of us and disappear. We worry about cars only a bit. Mostly we worry about the kids tripping or running into hidden fences. We never worry that they could disappear for good, snatched up, taken away.

Small groups appear out of the darkness, mostly people we know. The man who sits stone-still on his porch until the children are right upon him is always there, and they always scream when he lurches to life. The porch of our retired dentist is wrapped in cobwebs, and the kids get peanuts and sugarless gum. Uniformed sheriff deputies hand out candy through a small window in the department entryway. Stops at the homes of teachers are a must. Sometimes we walk in a cold mist. Sometimes we marvel at the stars the young ones never see in their quest for candy. A lot of ground is covered for what my children think is a lot of candy; they would be stunned by the efficient gathering and the volumes to be had on the well-lit, long, straight residential streets in the city.

Every year since our first was born 12 years ago, we have made our last stop on Halloween my parents' house. The kids ring the bell, call out "trick or treat," and thrill over the bowl my mom holds out the door as if it's the first candy of the night. Then they dash in to get their pictures taken and spill their riches on the floor for my father to examine and praise.

Last year, we left the village late. My oldest son had trick-or-treated on his own, and he and his friends wanted time to cover nearly the whole village. We had lingered over a glass of wine at a friend's house. It was a school night. My dad was understanding when I phoned from home saying we weren't going to stop this year, but the decision didn't sit right with any of us. The kids got back in their costumes and we piled into the car. When my mom came to the door, bowl in hand, her grandchildren shouted, "Trick or treat!" It wasn't too late after all. My mother got the camera and poured cider. My father got down on his hands and knees, with a bit more effort than 12 years before, and pretended as he always does to choose the biggest candy bar from each. With cries of protest and my dad's gentle laugh, the negotiations began.

I loved Halloween as a child, mostly for the candy. As a parent, I've rather dreaded it, mostly for the candy. And I'm not clever enough to hang witches in trees nor handy enough to stitch heirloom costumes. But the sense of order, of completion, that got its arms around my children and their grandparents that night, and the lingering sense of friends and stars and the dark, winding streets, made me think that it really does take a village.

passages

I once had a live snowy owl as a touchstone. Small and silent and seemingly carved of pure white marble, this owl allowed me to pass on skis at least once each winter, my eyes wandering back each time to see if he'd moved a feather. He never had.

At first I was merely elated when my husband told me in hushed tones to look slowly toward the lower branches on my right. But the owl's presence came to mean something more than just elation after the first winter or two; his presence made me slow down and feel lucky and grateful and awed.

The owl lived, at least on the days we saw him, on land behind our first house, a farmhouse nestled against a sumac-covered hillside from which we skied out our backdoor. Every winter weekend we loaded the woodstove, strapped on our skis and marched and herringboned our way up the slope. Some days the snow was so thick we couldn't see the top of the hill; on others the sun was so piercing we'd have our jackets unzipped by the time we reached the top.

We'd pause at the peak's small meadow perch to look out over the landscape that lay draped like a patchwork quilt in a hundred shades of brown along Lake Michigan's shoreline. From that perch we could see what weather was blowing in past the islands in the big lake and, if we were lucky, we could watch heavy clouds dumping snow even before they reached the shoreline. Sometimes the roar of the wind off the lake was so loud we couldn't hear each other speak. But as we ducked onto the narrow deer path, camouflaged among the evergreen branches as effectively as any castle's secret door, the world became instantly silent.

The path the deer created wound down through thick, fawn-colored brambles that caught at our legs, and then, once we hit the clearing below, we were on into hundreds of acres of hardwoods. We often chose to ski one of the many abandoned logging roads that ran through meadows, over hillsides and past seemingly ancient orchards of apple trees whose limbs, coated in a green-black fungus, looked like the gnarled fingers of a crone. These two small orchards had once supplied two homesteads now long gone; the corner of one crumbled grey stone foundation was all that was left. Still, the trees blossomed thinly in the spring and produced small, hard, sour apples each fall, some of which lingered on the snow-covered branches as if waiting for grateful hands to pick them.

It was only fitting that it was my husband who spotted the owl the first time. He is the one who pauses endlessly on the trail to examine scat at the base of a tree or the scratch marks upon a trunk that appear to me to be frantic, but I'm told are crafted with purpose. It's my husband who ponders over the varieties of winterberries and splits open pods left dangling and dormant from the fall. Left to my own devices, I would have seen little of it. I'm the one quickly lost to the blended sights and sounds of the woods in winter, falling into a reverent, meditative pace that has me slowing my breaths to the creaking trees and gazing wistfully at the mosaics the wind has made upon the face of the snow.

The snowy owl was on a low branch, close enough to the ground that from our angle his snowy feathers were easily lost in the white horizon beyond him. The owl was impossible to read. There was no flight in panic or annoyance. There was no bobbing of his head or obvious show of power by spreading his wings. He didn't blink or even gaze away. In fact, it was I who looked away first, and I wondered at the time if the owl knew that meant he had won. We leaned upon our ski poles for a moment and watched him, so small but gloriously regal and unflappable. I wondered if I had laid my hand upon his breast, would his heart have been beating wildly?

We saw him off and on for three more years, rarely in the same tree but always in the same field—what I assume was his chosen hunting ground, filled with unwitting hares and rodents. But even before we moved 13 years ago, that owl had gone. At the start I imagined him winging his way to the tundra, but as time passed I accepted that he'd died on the landscape somewhere, hopefully making it to the old age of nine or ten.

In my daydreams, I like to believe he found a mate and some descendent of theirs lives on in those fields. That vision has become one of my touchstones, reminding me that with all the wonderful and challenging changes happening Up North, there will always be those of us who need to know it's possible to put on our skis and sneak through a hidden passageway made by deer into a world where a silent snowy owl might let us pass.

keeping summer hours

Some people get kids who sleep in. We didn't. Our four kids were out of bed by 6:00 a.m. no matter what time they went to bed. Their curls may have been rumpled, their eyes groggy, but they were ready to start the day. And the only sign they'd stayed up later than usual was that they were increasingly cranky as the day went on. And so were we.

Thus, when you have "early risers" you tend to be committed to early bedtimes. No matter the season or circumstance, our kids were in bed by 8:00 p.m. Obviously, this was particularly challenging during summer nights when the sun outside their bedroom windows rivaled that at midday. Boats buzzed by on the lake, and just the sound of their motors conjured up visions of some adventure yet to be had before the sun went down. My husband or I would read until one by one our children fell asleep. Then he and I would sit on a quiet dock and watch the setting sun turn our world on the lake the color of magic.

One summer, when our oldest was eight, our next-door neighbor's young grandchildren arrived. That night, as I sat reading to the kids in their beds, the windows wide open to capture a breeze, we listened to the grandchildren playing baseball. Next, we heard them race to the lake shouting for towels on the way, and squealing as they leapt off the dock and into the water. It wasn't long before we heard one of them call a request to their grandparents to bring marshmallows to the bonfire.

When we first heard those children's voices, I began to shift uncomfortably in my chair. By the call for marshmallows, the evening glee playing out next door was a kind of torture for all of us. I looked up from the book to faces of pure longing as my kids gazed out the windows from their beds. When we heard the splashes of the grandchildren going into the lake a second time, I shut the book. "Okay," I said. "Hop up. Grab your swimsuits."

And that was that. Since that night we've lived whole lifetimes after 8:00 p.m. in the summer. Hundreds of bags of marshmallows have been consumed, and countless games of Capture the Flag have played themselves out until it is too dark to know your own teammates. I've watched as the bodies silhouetted on the swim raft are mere shadows on the horizon as they leap against the last light of the day. We've glided through water so still it mirrors our smiles, bundled in sweatshirts as the light turns us all bronze and gracefully opens a mosaic of color in our path ahead. We've cooked dinner over the bonfire night after night, starting to cook only when kids say they're hungry and heading into the house only for a forgotten ingredient. We've gazed at the face of the moon through the telescope at the edge of the water and drifted silently in the dark, in the middle of the lake, engulfed in a sea of stars.

At some point each summer, as I watch life unfolding in the stunning landscape of Up North on a summer night, I remember the night we let our kids get out of bed. Now, as our kids hurry to the boat so they can wakeboard across the glass calm of a sunset's remnants, I remember how we laughed watching those little kids scramble out of bed that night, pulling off their pajamas before their feet even hit the ground. When I listen now to the softer, sleepy dialogue as the night makes our world around the fire very small, and my daughter crawls in my lap, I remember the utter contentment we felt as our tired and happy kids finally returned to their beds that night.

"Hop up. Grab your suits," has become a part of our family lore. And for me, it's a kind of mantra. I'm reminded that while there are places in all our lives where sticking to a schedule and a plan is a must, summer nights Up North simply can't be one of them. Let it go. From the moment you allow yourself to simply drift on a mirrored lake at sunset or lie down on the beach to watch a brilliant night sky, you will feel at peace. The world will stop for just a while.

"Hop up. Grab your suits" and leave your scheduled world behind. You will feel wonder. And peace. And joy. And you will know, in that moment, there is simply nowhere else you need to be.

sanctuary

There is peace to be found in December Up North. The world becomes a refuge unto itself as oversized flakes drift to earth, laying pale blankets over the battered remains of November's winds and rains. Every small town and village glows in white lights, and tires are muffled as they pass slowly down main streets. People who wander this landscape in December, even for a weekend, understand that they have found a place to breathe, where life stands still in joy and quiet sanctuary.

In our small village, people gather on a December night in the village green to sing and stomp feet against the cold and watch for Santa, who arrives in the cab of the volunteer fire engine. Kids who have been chasing each other throughout the green dash to the road to wave and then race behind the truck to the old community center where Santa sits in a large chair in the center of the old wooden floor, and local women dressed as elves lay out cookies to be decorated with colored icing and Red Hots.

In December, snow clings to pitch-black tree limbs, forming intricate mosaics in our headlights as we rush down a country road to the Christmas concert at our children's school. We float through the glowing, hush-quiet village and turn at the small post office, a hub during the day. Two blocks up, just past the Lutheran church, the school that houses all four of our kids—now second grade to tenth—radiates with warmth. One of the boys begs our daughter to sing her song as she sits forward, trying not to wrinkle the bow on the back of her dress.

I choose a trail to ski that winds along the beach on a day framed in cornflower blue skies. I pop off my skis and walk to the water's edge, throwing a stick down the shore for our dog, Foxy, who skids and slides along the frozen sand. The breeze is light and refreshing, and I linger until I begin to chill. A couple passes me as I'm putting my skis back on, and the woman asks if I'm not afraid to be out in the woods alone. I say no and think to myself that being in the woods on this day is the antidote to fear.

> We float through the glowing, hush-quiet village.

We wake in the dark to the odd winter quiet that causes us to whisper as we light the fire and sip coffee, watching the windows framed in blown crystals. Kids with sleepy eyes and mussed hair wander down to the couch, and I sometimes get to hear daydreams in the moments just before the sun is up.

And on it goes. In December Up North it is easy to imagine that the world is at peace. It seems infinitely possible that the stars burning so brightly in our winter sky are bringing equal wonder and joy the world over. The sense of peace and goodwill is so pervasive that you can almost convince yourself that kids throughout the world go to sleep curled under quilts in houses that stand stoically against the wind, gathering snow upon their eaves just to make it all a bit more picture perfect.

But the world isn't at peace. Lives are not being lived nestled under quilts or standing upon the beach in a surprisingly gentle winter breeze. And when I confront the fact that I am helpless to change that truth, one of the things I fall back on is something I know I can do—I work a bit harder to preserve the things in our landscape that provide sanctuary for those who make their way Up North.

People have always needed what the landscape of Northern Michigan provides, for a week or for a lifetime—and certainly the world needs it now. Up North is a place to revive and regroup, to grieve and make peace, to find community and to learn to not be afraid.

Those of us who live this life and who love this sanctuary know its power. We were drawn by the dream of Up North, and because of that simple truth we now hold the future of this region in our hands. We are the caretakers of a place—a place that has the power to change lives, to splash smiles on the faces of children and to bring a bit of peace to the challenging lives of adults.

It's almost easy to think the world is at peace in December Up North. And that, quite simply, is a gift we have to give.

waves of
enchantment

We are among the people found on every lake who don't take their dock out until "the last possible moment." Our boat waits stoically in its hoist, and the kayaks are still stowed at the shoreline long after the leaves are gone.

More times than I'd share here I've stood shivering at the boat launch a mile from our house, shielding my eyes against the snow coming at me horizontally, trying to catch a glimpse of my husband, Neal, and our boat. One year he emerged like a phantom from a blinding snow that swirled along the lake's surface in a funnel pattern, his face nearly frostbitten, both of us realizing in an instant that he was literally upon the launch's dock.

But all who understand the concept of "the last possible moment" forgive us our foolishness. For truly, there is little that can compare to being in your boat on a lake gone quiet. We drift about enthralled by a lake that becomes almost all our own. We marvel at the colors of the shore and the sky mirrored on its surface. We relish the stark beauty that comes with an unexpectedly warm day after the leaves are gone.

But there was a time in my life when the gift of drifting on a perfectly still lake in the colors of October became something much more than just a delightful way to pass a few hours. One afternoon, over a decade ago, I was walking with a friend when I became suddenly very ill. It turned out to be a blood infection I'd gotten from breast-feeding my then five-month-old son, Austin. It was a nasty infection to cure, and I was hospitalized for several days. I had a

magazine to run and three children under five, but when I got home from the hospital I had absolutely no energy.

After I'd been home for a few weeks, we woke one weekend to a perfectly still autumn morning that was like living on the edge of heaven. We took coffee and blankets onto the dock to get closer to the canvas. But once there, I closed my eyes and turned my face to the sun.

When Neal suggested a ride in the boat I was resistant, my limbs heavy with the constant fatigue and with the warmth of the blanket and the sun. But when I saw the confusion on the faces of my children as they looked at me from the boat now readied—yet another excursion without me—I rallied enough to climb on. I went to the bow of the boat and wrapped the baby and myself in the blanket.

Neal motored quietly into deeper water and then turned to head peacefully along the shoreline. From my perch at the front of the boat, I could watch as the bow interrupted the mosaics on the lake's surface and sent gentle, silent ripples of color in its wake. It was as if I was seeing the world anew: The trees aflame with red and gold, the big, cornflower blue sky dotted with bulbous, white clouds, the shorelines of cottages swept clean of summer's toys and prepared for the season to come.

I looked back at my husband seated in the driver's seat behind our five-year-old who was lost in concentration at what he believed was the charge of driving the boat. I held the pant leg of my two-year-old who peered just over the bow, proclaiming with wild enthusiasm the many wonders he could see below us, some real, some not. The baby lay against my chest, but as would be his approach to life, he'd wiggled until he was face out, greeting the wind head on, his eyes watering, his toothless, lopsided grin never wavering.

And just like that, I began to heal. Not the momentary high kind of healing, but healing that started with conviction and moved steadily forward. It was, I told a few people at the time, like an enchantment, a kind of healing that seemed to begin from the spirit out.

Since then, whenever I look about Northern Michigan and see houses where the dock is still standing in October or watch a canoe gliding silently past in autumn's colors, I know them to be people who will always wait for "that last possible moment." I know we share the belief it's always worth waiting for one last chance to drift into enchantment.

earflaps and a bathrobe

We run into them on trails and ski hills all over Northern Michigan; people clad in matching, dazzling Lycra or sleek, color-coordinated downhill outfits.

Then there are the rest of us, the people who live a snow culture, day in, day out. We like to think our look is sort of avante-garde L.L. Bean, especially on a bad hair day. That's because it's tough to maintain all the pieces of what once constituted a pulled-together look. A few long winters and time takes its toll. Substitutions get made. Before you know it, you've got an eclectic mix of L.L. Bean, Woolrich, Farm and Fleet, Wild Kingdom and 18th century Eskimo. It isn't pretty, but function we've got down.

When you live with snow for four or five months out of the year, you tend to think less about how you look and a lot more about how you want to feel. That would be warm. It's true that when you first start dressing with function in mind, you hope you don't run into people who dress with an eye to fashion. But after a while, you simply don't care. And that's when it can get scary.

Brad Pitt couldn't look good in this hat

For instance, Neal has this hat. It's a warm hat. It's a big hat. It has earflaps and a Velcro attachment under the chin that he regularly attaches. Now Neal's a handsome guy, but Brad Pitt couldn't look good in this hat. Trust me. And when he adds his Carhartts, his 10-year-old Patagonia jacket, his Sorels and some snowmobile mitts recommended by the guy at the hardware store, let's just say we aren't invited in much. The only thing more disconcerting than Neal

 in that hat is me in that hat, particularly a few years ago when I'd regularly wear it going for wood at 6 a.m. in my bathrobe, Sorels and fireplace mittens. It was a blessing for all concerned when we stopped heating with wood.

I was in college when I discovered cross-country skiing and the art of layering. My first years in the sport I looked darn good, having invested in a pair of black insulated tights, a purple-and-black shell and even a hat to match. A few years later, on maybe the fifth night I had my puppy Sara home, she chewed a hole in the knee of my tights. And it was at a Lake Michigan bonfire in October one year that I singed the sleeve of my shell. The hat is long gone, but I still wear that combo cross-country skiing, my pink long underwear shining through at the knee.

Our boys are pulling us back to the downhill ski world, a place neither Neal nor I have been much since high school. Not wanting to invest in clothes and equipment right away, we took to the slopes in our worse-for-wear cross-country gear, including the skis. We were strangers from a faraway land. And because you don't move quite the same way when you downhill, it doesn't take long to discover you need layers on top of your cross-country gear to stay warm. By the time we were through we resembled Mr. and Mrs. Michelin helping the boys maneuver the bunny hill. During the few winters I added being very pregnant to that get-up, I actually frightened a few small children. As a favor to everyone, the next year we each got a pair of downhill ski pants. The year after, we bought snazzy downhill mittens. We're hoping eventually for a timeless look, undoubtedly the closest we'll come to being fashionable on the slopes.

There are places where we feel right at home. Out on the ice, for instance. Ice fishing, now there's a world unconcerned with fashion. Carhartts and snowmobile suits (black, with none of those reflector strips) prevail. Of course, most of the time you never know what they're wearing: the fishermen in the shanties in front of our house are known to us mostly as friendly or grouchy or enthusiastic voices, coming from tiny windows.

Occasionally, the mostly men inside beckon my brightly colored little guys, and Neal—well, we've discussed Neal—into their shanties to peer down the hole in the ice. They always go. After a few moments they stumble back out, the boys shielding their eyes against the bright light of day. Neal isn't shielding his eyes. He's wearing his very large (they're actually designed to fit comfortably over eyeglasses), black, sort of square, wraparound trout-fishing sunglasses. The effect is as if he's recovering from eye surgery. Truth be known, I've actually tried to throw them out. Twice. Even I have my limits.

cold praise

Winter's palette is not easily defined. Images and emotions are defined, in part, by their wild fluctuation. And therein lies some of its intrigue. Jet-black branches of trees, naked and exposed for the winter, become more art than function. A cornflower blue sky is a reason for conversation; not a summer given, rather a gift. The creaking of a hardwood, a slight exhale, the hollow echo of a whoop from the one who has skied on ahead are often the only sounds that define an afternoon. There are smiles no one sees.

Spending any real time in Northern Michigan in the winter means making peace with the unknown. Embracing both the fury and the hush. There's an understanding that life runs the gamut: awe, adventure, introspection, a sense of warmth—sometimes a good dose of fear. Winter evenings with family and friends can be among the most communal of the year. But often, winter is a more personal journey. And the winter wind howling against our windows reminds us that there are many kinds of security in life, some simpler to achieve than others: a soft down comforter, faces still slightly windburned, a book that never seems to leave its place by the fire, a woodpile well covered.

We choose to be here in the winter because we are looking for life to be different. And we thrive when we remember to let that be true. It's about having the luxury of a moonlight ski when the full moon happens to fall on a Tuesday. Carving the first slow s-curves into the powdered slopes of a local ski resort on a Wednesday evening. Stomping the snow off your boots just as you open the door to a coffeehouse and are met with that rush of pure, aromatic warmth. Offering an interested customer a cup of tea and being pleasantly surprised when the bell over the door interrupts your conversation. Coming upon a snowy owl 50 yards into the woods when you surely ought to be getting dinner started. Walking back from the mailbox at night, your home all aglow, the air so clear and cold it makes you catch your breath, a small stream of chimney smoke dancing against a star-laden sky.

Winter slows life down for us. And when we are at our best, we adjust our expectations. We strive for a true balance between what we sometimes ask this place to be and what it so easily is. It is achingly beautiful. It is visceral. It is as honest as we let it be. It is so much fun. It is filled with creative spirit that thrives when we honor the core of what this place is about. And if we let it, life in Northern Michigan always leads us quietly back to those things we want to value most.

in search of bluegills

One balmy night last summer two of my sons and a friend commandeered the kitchen preparing for their first solo fishing trip on the lake. It was a process shaped both by the coiled energy of preadolescent males and the orderliness of the men they would one day be. More food was packed than could be eaten in a day much less during an excursion that would surely end with the arrival of midmorning's hot sun. They fell asleep talking about fish to be caught and the reliability of alarm clocks.

The lake at dawn was glass-still, just a slight quiver running down its spine. I hugged myself—against the cold, ostensibly—and watched as our oldest, Ben, 11, our second, Peter, 8, and their pal loaded gear and rations into the boat, which, at 10 feet and light enough to hoist on a couple of shoulders, seemed suddenly entirely too small. The motor, however, loomed large and too powerful. This was the first time Ben would take the boat out of sight, into the channel at the end of our lake where the marshes make for great bluegill fishing.

They took off, Peter waving back at us enthusiastically, Ben's gaze locked on the course before him. I could hear the prop cutting the water long after I could make out the curve of their faces, the shape of Ben's slim back tense with the drama of the morning.

If the gift of a boat had begun a rite of passage, then this trip, over a year later, was its completion. Neal and I had wanted to find something for Ben's 10th birthday that might represent new freedom and the responsibility that comes with it. The idea of a small boat that each of our children would earn the right to drive alone at age 10 came out of my own experience. I had been 10 years old myself the first time I climbed into the scarred, impossibly heavy rowboat that came with the first cottage my family rented. My older siblings lived in the other boat, a turquoise and white speedboat that pulled kids from all over the lake on water skis, sometimes six at a time if there were an audience. That old rowboat had been my shot at some kind of freedom.

At the start of that summer, my mom stood on the end of the dock with me pointing to liquid landmarks, defining my boundaries by the color of the water. Dark, almost black was absolutely off limits. I know now how torn she must have been wanting to create a large enough arena in which I could feel some sense of adventure, but seeing all that could go wrong for a child alone on the lake. As for me, I saw nothing but possibility.

Now there I was, the parent left standing on the dock. On the kids' behalf, I felt elation. And some kind of sadness: time had come for adventures without me. And that was as it should be.

Neal and I began looking for their return around 10 a.m., asking each other only occasionally if we thought they were all right, laughing about how much they'd probably eaten. Sometime about an hour later, I picked them out on the horizon and we walked, didn't run, to the dock. There's a glow that takes over children's faces when joy has got hold of them. And there it was. I could feel it, down to my bones.

They tumbled out of the boat, falling over each other's sentences as they shared the story of what had, in fact, been a small crisis. The motor had died, and Ben hadn't been able to restart it. They had rowed toward shore until their arms ached and got close enough for Peter to jump overboard in his life jacket and swim to shore. While Ben kept working on the motor, Peter found a kind man who helped them get the boat to shore and discovered they'd let a rope tangle in the prop. He cut the rope out, saw the motor restarted and wished them well.

The food was all gone. There were no fish. What they were left with, what we all were left with, was the knowledge that in the face of a real challenge they'd survived perfectly well on their own.

Ben had wanted a Gameboy for his 10th birthday. Actually, he'd wanted a Gameboy for every birthday since six. We knew he'd rather have had a Gameboy than the right to drive a small fishing boat, but he'd been gracious in his disappointment. I remembered that on an evening after the fishing trip as he took the boat for the last spin of the day in a light so beautiful it made my heart ache. I watched his blond head glow in a world turned gold, and for a little while I could make out the name he'd carefully lettered on the transom with his father a few nights after his birthday: "Gameboy."

a place to heal

On the Sunday after September 11, I walked through the woods with my family. Four blond heads ran ahead of Neal and me, laughing at jokes we couldn't hear and lying in wait to scare us. They marveled at the monarch cocoon Neal found and the snakeskin shed long ago. They fought over walking sticks, and two of them stubbed toes on the same protruding root as they ran down the biggest hill and took nasty falls. It all felt so normal, except perhaps the firmness with which I held each of their hands off and on as we passed in and out of shafts of sunlight that seeped through the forest canopy.

People heal in different ways and in their own time. But there are those of us who, at times like this, need to step outside what man has created, step away from what mankind does to one another. We find peace and the will to heal in the quiet of the woods, in the meditation of a silent lake or the powerful winds sweeping into the dunes high above Lake Michigan. For us, in these places it's easier to replace an overwhelming sense of helplessness with the inspiration to contribute whatever and wherever we can. It's easier to remind ourselves that the world is better than the evil of a few and the sky we lie looking at is the sky shared by everyone on this planet. There is a universal spirit to that which no man created. There is peace. And there is the power to heal.

slam of the screen door

It was my first summer Up North and I lay stretched across the plank seat of our old aluminum rowboat, a book propped on my stomach. The sinking sun was still warm, the lapping on the sides of the boat so lulling that I drifted off to sleep. When a slightly cooler breeze nudged me awake, I opened my eyes to find I was in the midst of a glorious sunset, part of a canvas of blazing light and illusion. The sky and its clouds existed in two universes, one above me and one I could reach out and touch in the dead-still water. Everything was bathed in an ethereal light, turning even my fingers a deep red clay color as I reached for small diamonds of light tossed here and there on the water.

I was 10 years old and experiencing, for the first time, what it means to be all alone, surrounded by the splendor of nature. I pulled my knees to my chest to stop my heart from exploding and looked for other boats. There were none. This spectacle had been created just for me. I felt huge and oddly powerful. At the same time, I felt small and inconsequential and more than once glanced back toward the cottage lights that had begun to peek through the trees.

What eventually prompted me to dip the heavy oars into the blackened water and head toward shore that night escapes me. Maybe it was the slam of a screen door, or the promise of laughter and comfort found in the cottage's small, shadowy rooms awash in yellow light. I dragged the heavy boat as far as I could onto the marshy shore and, leaving the sun's last light behind me, started up the darkened path.

the magic wand had been waved

As I entered the cottage that night, I might have been met with an invitation to join a card game, or an inquisitive smile from my mom as I headed to the daybed on the screen porch to read the book I kept in only that spot. Regardless of what greeted me, I didn't try to put into words what I'd experienced. It was a summer of many unspoken discoveries—some about myself, some about us as a family. I don't know if I thought speaking of them would diminish them or whether I feared that words would somehow break the wondrous spell we were all living under.

It was a spell, as sure as any I had been served in my regular doses of fairy tales. It began when, without explanation or preamble, my mom let us live like children of the forest, eating whenever we liked, bathing in the lake. The magic wand had been waved and it no longer mattered that a meal with all five food groups made it to the table at a certain time each night. We ate simply, straight from my grandmother's repertoire. Fresh cucumbers in vinegar. Tomato sandwiches with mayonnaise. Fried egg sandwiches, egg salad on toast or leftover deviled eggs. We devoured bowl upon bowl of strawberries dipped in confectioners' sugar. On weekends, when my father was up, some meat was grilled, some corn boiled on the tiny stovetop indoors. On rare occasions we got Coca-Cola.

My mom helped us perfect the card games she had grown up playing endlessly with her mother and aunts: gin rummy, pinochle, the beginnings of bridge. She swam some. For one

whole week she made jellies, the air around the cottage soaked with the scent of boiling fruit, her arms stained to the elbow. And she read books. *Hawaii, The Crucible, Exodus,* thick books with stiff spines that I collected in her wake. My mom didn't read at home; she claimed if she started a book, she was never able to stop and then nothing got done. How lovely it was to see my mom with nothing to get done.

My dad would arrive on Friday nights, and from his car would spill our friends from home or, more slowly, my grandmother, my great aunts, my aunt. The Hatch women come North to spend a week or two, playing cards for pennies and drinking Vernor's or, when my dad was up, Moose Milk, his cocktail that had them all dancing through the house in a chain one New Year's Eve. The Hatch women loved my dad, one of the only men left on my mom's side of the family. They flirted with him to no end, and to their dying days, he flirted right back with each of them.

As the summer wore on, he emerged from the car looking increasingly worn. Detroit had begun to burn, and he was weary of military escorts to the hospital where he worked. He was devastated, as was my mother, that the city they loved would be so torn. Those evenings without houseguests passed quietly.

After that first summer, it was easy for me to believe all manner of good things happen Up North. We arrived teetering on the edge of innocence. My siblings were 13, 14 and almost 16. We'd passed many swell summers in our suburban neighborhood, but things were changing at home. There were floats to be built. Races to be won. Friendships to be nurtured well beyond the confines of our tree-lined street. Increasingly our daily lives unfolded without each other, our experiences tucked away, unshared. It seemed a whisper would blow my oldest sister completely to the other side of childhood and the others would tumble after her. As the youngest I knew that I would truly be left behind, until it was my time.

So it was a thrill for me when we climbed the narrow stairs to the cottage attic for the first time, and I saw the three double beds tucked between the eaves—one for each of us girls. At home I slept alone. Doors seemed increasingly to be closing in my face, and my sisters' voices had become the muffled sounds I struggled to hear through our adjoining bathroom door. In that

attic I sat perched on my own bed, all ears, utterly legitimate. On cold nights, my oldest sister would scurry about the creaky wood floor in her shorty nightgown, tucking extra quilts around my sister and me before standing unsteadily on her bed, pulling the cord on the light that swung overhead and diving under her own covers. The room would go so black you couldn't see your hand before your face, and I would drift off, timing my breaths to the cadence of theirs.

My bed lay at eye level next to a tiny window that, like all the cottage windows, had no window covering. I could watch the morning light reveal droplets of dew as they lay upon the leaves, and if I lounged, I could watch them dry before my eyes. I'd stay in bed until my stomach or the beauty of an unfolding day drove me from it, tiptoeing past my sleeping sisters. It would be hours before they woke. I'd dress at the bottom of the stairs. A swimsuit and then, as often as I could, the deep apricot T-shirt with navy stripes my brother had outgrown and put in the Goodwill box. I loved that T-shirt, worn so soft over the years that donning it was like slipping into a bed of rose petals. Best of all, it had been my brother's.

From the time I could walk, if my brother's light shone my way, I followed, and that summer was no different. Long gone were the days when I crept into his bedroom in the early morning light to breathe soft breaths upon his cheeks, willing him to wake. I had learned to feign indifference, most mornings barely looking away from the back of my cereal box as he entered the screen porch, wiping sleep from his eyes. There was no telling on which days he'd stand up,

stretch dramatically, then flash me a grin or maybe a casual nod, indicating I could come along. My eyes on his broad back, I would push my stride to match his and hope he didn't notice when I took small, hurried steps to keep up.

Once underway, if he wanted me to leap, I gave it a try. In exchange, I learned how to walk as quietly as a Native American through the forest and to prime the motor on the old boat. I learned to water ski on one ski when he decided I should—he simply didn't throw me a second ski. I was angry that afternoon, when after what seemed like hours, I pulled myself up the ladder of the boat, the muscles in my pencil-thin arms quivering. I asked him why he put me through that and he grinned, saying simply, "I knew you could do it. And I knew you'd love it."

We were often long gone when my sisters decided the day should begin. They were devoted water-skiers and practiced their water ballet routines endlessly, determined to outdo the performers at Cypress Gardens and especially those Weeki Wachee girls. But they were moving beyond the age of playing all day. They increasingly liked to sit. In the sun. At some point nearly every day they would lead a group of girls to our swimming raft for the express purpose of sunbathing and gossiping. They would slip carefully off the dock, one by one, squealing as the water level reached stomachs exposed by their new two-piece suits. With one hand they held towels on their heads filled with suntan lotion, shampoo, magazines, stationery and lemon juice for lightening their hair—someone carried the small transistor radio.

I cavorted beside them like a dolphin, the clay and mud bottom sending shivers down my spine every time my toes dug in. I would slide under the water and navigate the green waters, popping my head up between the rusted oil drums that held the raft afloat. The sound of my breath was enormous, the world an eerie green. The noise above me echoed slightly as the girls laughed and daydreamed and practiced the lyrics to "Ain't No Mountain High Enough," drowning out the static of the transistor. It was their laughter, resonating against the metal of the steel drums, which finally would draw me back into the sunshine.

There's a laziness to laughter when you think there's plenty of time for more. And we always lived as if there was time. The end of summer caught us by surprise, even though it had begun to make itself known—darkness coming upon us before we were ready, the breeze making us reach for sweaters. Suddenly the rooms were too neat, the waterfronts too empty, the world suddenly gone quiet. It was time to go home. We'd wander the rooms, sit on the empty dock, lingering as if around a bonfire that only smolders—the night and the cold nudge you to move on, the memories and the discoveries won't let you leave.

A few weeks ago, I woke to the sound of rain in the middle of the night. As I was shutting the windows in the bedroom our three boys share, I noticed the full moon glistening on the lake; the water shimmered, a sea of jewels. I realized the sound that woke me was not a summer rain, just the steady rustling of leaves on the gracious old ash outside our bedroom windows.

I stood for a moment in the cool breeze coming through the screens. The night air was familiar, rich and damp, so like nights at the cottage when my oldest sister would pull old coverlets and quilts over me before she scurried barefoot through the cool to her own double bed. The same moon, the same breeze, the same glistening water—I could have been 10 years old again were it not for the three little bodies tucked under comforters covered in clouds.

But I'm the mom Up North now, waving from the dock as the kids drive back and forth in the neighbor's dinghy with its 5-horsepower motor pretending they are pirates on the high seas, yet never more than 20 yards from our dock. It's me who oohs and aahs over the legions of sculptures made from natural clay they found by the stream and then tries to figure out what to do with them. I send juice up to the fort, shuffle cards, latch life jackets, team up for baseball, anchor the kayak, make temporary homes for frogs and caterpillars (but not yet snakes), and snuggle warm little bodies at bonfires.

Now it's my children's laughter that floats up to the house as they play King of the Mountain on the swimming raft and clean their berry-stained faces with a leap into the lake. Through my husband, a child of East Coast salt marshes, I discover anew this place I've loved for so long. I see him fish the Manistee for the first time, find his first morel and introduce his parents to the lake. And in the peace of summer Sundays, my mom and dad now sit in the shade of our huge hemlocks, chatting with their grown children, delighting in the treasures brought by grandchildren. At times, she is his eyes; he is her ears at others.

Sometimes I find myself on the dock, alone as the sun is setting, the voices of my family and friends floating down from the porch. In those moments, I can hear my father's gentle laugh drift through that first screen porch and see my brother's dancing brown eyes. I smell the bath powder of the Hatch women and see my sisters' graceful procession to the raft. I feel the peace as my mom drifted off, her book resting on her lap.

I lie down and reach my hand, red as clay, to touch small diamonds of light tossed here and there on the water. I am home.

Prism Publications, Inc.
148 E. Front Street
Traverse City, MI 49684
231-941-8174
www.traversemagazine.com
Printed and bound in Canada
Cover and text designed by Angela Saxon,
Saxon Design, Inc, Traverse City, MI

Library of Congress Cataloguing-in-Publication Data
Fellows, Deborah Wyatt.
Reflections of a life up north / by Deborah Wyatt
Fellows. -- 2nd ed. -- Traverse City, MI :
Prism Publications, 2007.

p. ; cm.

Includes index of photographers.
ISBN: 0918293006

1. Fellows, Deborah Wyatt. 2. Authors and publishers--
Michigan. 3. Periodicals--Publishing--Michigan.
4. Michigan--Description and travel. 5. Michigan--
Pictorial works. 6. Nature photography--Michigan.
I. Title.

F572.N7 F45 2004   2004092478
917.74/9--dc22   0405

Photo Credits:

Thaddius Bedford: 160

Steve Brimm: 137

Kathleen Dodge Bühler: i, ix, x, 5, 7, 8-9, 20, 21, 40b,
42, 44b, 50, 56, 67, 68, 69, 76, 77, 78, 79, 80a, 80c, 89,
93, 103, 107, 117, 147, 149, 157, 163

Brian Confer: 129, 138

Dembinsky Photo Associates
  E.R. Degginger: 24
  Bill Leman: 140a
  Dick Scott: 66
  Joe Sroka: 128

Glen Graves: 38, 91, 96-97

Brian and Shawn Malone: 126

Patrick Wellever: 132b

Traverse, Northern Michigan's Magazine

Sabrina Burton: 40c, 94a, 162c

Brian Confer: cover, iii, vi, viii, xii, 1, 10, 11, 13, 14b,
14c, 16, 19, 22-23, 26b, 26c, 27, 31, 36, 40a, 41, 43, 44a,
44c, 45, 46, 48, 49, 52, 53, 58, 60b, 61, 63, 64, 71, 72, 74,
80b, 81, 82, 86-87, 92, 94b, 94c, 100, 111, 112a, 112b,
113, 114, 116c, 118, 120-121, 122, 123, 141, 142, 144,
146, 148, 150, 153, 154, 158-159, 160, 162a, 162b, 164b

Thomas Kachadurian: 106

Keith King: 60a

Matt McCormick: 116a

Leigh Patton: 6, 26a, 30c, 146a, 151

Chad Phinney: 18, 37, 59, 116b, 164a

Nile Young Jr.: iv, 2, 12, 32, 34, 70, 85

Todd Zawistowski: Author photo, ii, 4, 15, 28, 29, 30a,
35, 51, 62, 95, 98, 104, 109, 110, 112c, 125, 130, 132a,
132c, 133, 134, 135, 140b, 140c, 145, 152, 155